Authentic Assessments for the English Classroom

NCTE Editorial Board

Authentic Assessments for the English Classroom

Joanna Dolgin
East Side Community High School, New York City

Kim Kelly
East Side Community High School, New York City

Sarvenaz Zelkha
East Side Community High School, New York City

NCTE
National Council of Teachers of English
1111 W. Kenyon Road, Urbana, Illinois 61801-1096

Staff Editor: Carol Roehm
Interior Design: Jenny Jensen Greenleaf
Cover Design: Frank Cucciare, Blink Concept and Design, Inc.

NCTE Stock Number: 02329

It is the policy of NCTE in its journals and other publications to provide a forum for the open discussion of ideas concerning the content and the teaching of English and the language arts. Publicity accorded to any particular point of view does not imply endorsement by the Executive Committee, the Board of Directors, or the membership at large, except in announcements of policy, where such endorsement is clearly specified.

Every effort has been made to provide current URLs and email addresses, but because of the rapidly changing nature of the Web, some sites and addresses may no longer be accessible.

Library of Congress Cataloging-in-Publication Data

Dolgin, Joanna, 1981–
Authentic assessments for the English classroom / Joanna Dolgin, Kim Kelly, Sarvenaz Zelkha.
p. cm.
Includes bibliographical references and index.
ISBN 978-0-8141-0232-9 (pbk)
1. East Side Community High School (New York, N.Y.)—Case studies. 2. Educational tests and measurements—New York (State)—New York—Case studies. 3. Language arts (Secondry)—New York (State)—New York—Case studies. I. Kelly, Kim, 1973– II. Zelkha, Sarvenaz, 1976– III. Title.
LB3053.N7D65 2010
428.0071'27471—dc22

2010035321

Contents

INTRODUCTION vii

1 AUTHENTIC ASSESSMENT OF INDEPENDENT READING 1

CHAPTER 1 In the Middle School Classroom: Includes Tips on Valuable Resources, Conferencing, and Reading Plans 3

CHAPTER 2 Authentic Assessment of Independent Reading as a Graduation Requirement 19

2 ROUNDTABLES AND OTHER PERFORMANCE-BASED ASSESSMENTS 29

CHAPTER 3 The Middle School Roundtable 33

CHAPTER 4 The High School Roundtable 48

CHAPTER 5 Authentic Formative Assessments in the High School Classroom 62

CHAPTER 6 Where Do *You* Go from Here? 77

APPENDIX 83

WORKS CITED 135

INDEX 137

AUTHORS 141

Introduction

The middle of January every year:

"Ok, so, next week you guys will be taking the English Regents."

Groans.

"I know. I know, but it's something you have to pass to graduate high school. It's just a test of critical reading and writing and that is something you've all been doing all year."

Blank stares.

"So . . . it's a six-hour test, three hours each . . ."

"What?" A student interrupts.

"Six hours?" Another student interjects.

"Yes." I take a deep breath because, as a class, we have had this discussion more than once before, and I know where it will end. "Six hours. It is three hours each day and you have two days to take it."

"Six hours?"

"Yes, but over two days. Just think of it this way—they are giving you plenty of time to show your skills. Use the time to your advantage. Now . . ." As I continue to present the students with more pointers to approaching the test, I can feel their heartbeats quicken, see their pupils dilate, hear their breathing grow heavier.

One student who has yet to succumb to test anxiety asks a question. "So, is this test on the stuff we've been doing in class?"

I pause and think. "Yes and no."

"What does that mean?"

"It means, yes, it's on critical reading and writing, but no because they will give you all new texts to read and analyze on the exam. First you will listen to a passage and write a response, then you will read a nonfiction passage and write a response, then you will read two short literary pieces and write a response, and for the final part you will connect two books you have read to a quote they provide. So, you're really just flexing your writing muscles and your ability to think critically about different texts. And again, they give you a lot of time. . . ."

"So, all the stuff we have to read and write about on the test will be new to us?"

"Yes." I reply with a somewhat desperate smile in recognition of the anxiety that is spreading through the room.

There are myriad pressures associated with high-stakes standardized tests. These pressures affect students, teachers and their classrooms, and administrators. Students feel they are judged or labeled by tests alone. Teachers feel they are not trusted to adequately assess and evaluate their own students and curriculum. Administrators feel they must meet quotas in terms of passing rates and cutoffs so that the school is not labeled as failing (Kohn 27–29). All of this combines to create a dangerous environment that may lead schools away from authentic learning and assessment. It is our belief that it is possible to provide authentic and more nuanced definitions of success within schools. By authentic we mean assessments that are developed by teachers in conjunction with course curriculum, that provide students with clear feedback and understanding about their strengths and growth in English, that require higher-order thinking skills, and that hold students to high standards while rooted in real-world scenarios. We believe that, in addition to standardized tests, we should use assessments that allow students a variety of means to display their skills and to be held accountable for their weaknesses. Furthermore, these assessments provide teachers with an authentic way of gauging understanding in their classrooms and give administrators a more complete picture of the learning that happens in their school. Like Grant Wiggins, we believe that "assessment anchors teaching and authentic tasks anchor assessment" (7).

About Our School

East Side Community High School is a small 6–12 middle/high school located on the Lower East Side of Manhattan. Our mission is as follows: East Side Community High School is committed to the belief that all students can, must, and will learn. We set high standards for each student and help them meet these standards by providing personal attention, a safe and respectful environment, a strong sense of community, and a curriculum that is both challenging and engaging. Approximately 85 percent of our student body is eligible for free lunch. The racial breakdown is 60 percent Latino, 30 percent African American, and 10 percent white or Asian. Many of our students enter East Side as struggling readers and writers. Many of our students have or need an Individualized Education Plan. Other students could be labeled *gifted*. This reality makes it critical that we differentiate our teaching and promote the use of a wide variety of assessments, both within curricular units and at the end of a semester or year, so that all students can find an entry point to successful learning. Rather than relying solely on anxiety-inducing standardized tests, we provide more individualized ways for students to express their learning. They are able to express their knowledge in writing through an extensive cover letter that addresses the content of the class, as well as through a reflection on their own performance, or they can defend their ideas orally in the roundtable presentation.

In the spring of 2008, for the second year in a row, our school received a "well-developed" on our school quality review, an intensive onsite examination of the school conducted by outside professionals. In their review, some of their summative points were as follows:

- The school sets very high expectations for students' work habits and achievement through well-researched individual goals.
- The school is a powerful learning community directed to students' academic and social progress and very well supported by professional development.
- The school's priority goal for students to become readers is very successful and engenders an extraordinary love of books (New York City Department of Education, 2008).

In addition to this school quality review, the New York City Department of Education has given East Side an A on our school report card for both the middle and the high school each year since the report card system was implemented.

Because of the socioeconomic demographics of our school and our belief that education should be equal for all, we also find the research of Alfred Tatum highly useful because as he stresses the importance of relevant curriculum and authentic assessment. We agree with him that the achievement gap can be closed with socially accessible curricula (Tatum 54). Using backward planning and a curriculum focused on authentic assessment allows us to create units that are socially, politically, and emotionally relevant while equipping students with high academic as well as real-world skills. However, though Tatum's major focus of research is on young African American men, his ideas are applicable to all students no matter their race, class, gender, or location. We do not want intellectually challenging and authentic assessment just for students at East Side; we want this for all young people as we believe it will make for a stronger, more thoughtful, and more dynamic future for our country.

Educational equality is also one of the goals for standardized testing that is not working. While in theory standardized tests should reduce educational inequality, "In states where 'high-stakes testing' is the primary policy reform, disproportionate numbers of minority, low-income, and special needs students have failed tests for promotion and graduation, leading to grade retention, failure to graduate, and sanctions for schools, without efforts to ensure equal and adequate teaching, texts, curriculum, and other educational resources" (Darling-Hammond 1). This does not spell out educational equality, and we firmly believe a shift to more authentic means of assessment will do more to make educational equality a reality. This is an issue of great importance for our school and our nation. In the wake of No Child Left Behind, we find ourselves in "a situation in which what may have started out in some educators' and legislators' minds as an attempt to make things better, [but] in the end is all usually transformed into another set of mechanisms for social stratification" (Apple 198).

By choice, East Side is a member school of the New York Performance Standards Consortium (NYPSC). The consortium

> is a coalition of high schools across New York State which have pioneered the creation of educational communities synonymous with active student learning, exemplary professional development, and innovative curriculum and teaching strategies for 21st century students. . . . Consortium schools have devised a system of assessment which consists of eight components including alignment with state standards, professional development, external review, and formative and summative data. Consortium schools have documented how their work meets and exceeds New York State Regents standards through a system of rigorous commencement-level performance-based assessment tasks. (*Alternatives to High-Stakes Testing*, www.performanceassessment.org)

Ample data have been compiled by external committees and school reviews sponsored by the Department of Education to assess the effectiveness of this approach. In New York City, the overall dropout rate is 38.9 percent, whereas it is only 9.9 percent at consortium schools. Citywide acceptance rate to college is 62 percent, whereas at consortium schools it is 91 percent (*FAQs*, www.performanceassessment.org). Through use of performance-based assessments such as roundtables with portfolio review, screenplay panel presentations, and independent reading exit projects that will be outlined in this book, East Side has become one of these schools that experiences success with low dropout rates and high college acceptance rates.

In the *Educational Leadership* article "Measuring What Matters," Mike Schmoker questions the validity of standardized testing while promoting the work being done in the consortium—the group of schools in New York City to which East Side belongs that promote alternative assessment. The reality is that "schools and even whole states could make steady gains on standardized tests without offering students intellectually challenging tasks" (Schmoker 71). This, too, is critical to the decision to begin to incorporate more alternative or authentic forms of assessment in the classroom. It is our belief that we should not settle for gains in standardized testing if it means that students are not being challenged intellectually. While the push for standardized tests was supposed to improve standards, it has actually served to lower them. "States and districts that have relied primarily on test-based accountability, emphasizing sanctions for students, have often produced greater failure rather than greater success for their most educationally vulnerable students" (Darling-Hammond 2). Research has shown that standardized tests narrow the curriculum, push instruction to lower-order cognitive thinking skills, and lead to distortion of scores (Klein, Hamilton, McCaffrey, & Stecher; Koretz and Barron; Linn).

Although East Side is a consortium school that is exempt from most New York State Regents exams, all students are still required to take some standardized tests. All students must take the high-stakes, state-mandated English language arts (ELA) tests in middle school and high school to be promoted and/or graduate. However, we stand firm in our philosophy that if teachers are creating challenging curricula with authentic assessment, then our students will be well equipped with the skills to master any state exam as well as be prepared for college. In the sixth, seventh, and eighth grades, students must take a state-mandated standardized ELA exam that rates them from Level One (the lowest) to Level Four (the highest). By the end of eighth grade, 59 percent of students score a Level Two and 35 percent score a Level Three. The next required state English exam is in January of eleventh grade. On average, more than 80 percent of students pass the comprehensive English Regents on their first try, and 100 percent pass within three attempts. Beyond just passing, on average, more than 65 percent score above a 75. Though we experience success on standardized tests, our intent is never to "teach to the test."

For us, the opinion of the parents regarding student learning is paramount. In a 2006 Gallup Poll, only 17 percent of parents believed standardized tests were a valid measure of student learning, whereas in a survey of more than 800 consortium parents, only 8 percent thought so. The consortium survey also stated that 93 percent of parents preferred teacher assessment, compared to only 39 percent that trusted testing corporations' assessments. Ninety-two percent of parents trusted the child's teacher to prepare the student for college-level work, and 95 percent believed their child's teachers had a good idea of their child's strengths and weaknesses (*Parent Survey*, www.performanceassessment.

org). Parents' trust in teachers over standardized tests is a cornerstone of our philosophy. Though the mandates of No Child Left Behind may have presented hope through standardized tests, it has become clear over the past six years that "NCLB rests on false assumptions—e.g., test scores equal educational quality" (*No Child Left Behind After Six Years: An Escalating Track Record of Failure*, http://www.fairtest.org). Through the networking of Fair Test.org, more than 150 education, civil rights, religious, and other organizations have signed the joint organizational statement calling for an overhaul of No Child Left Behind that moves the law away from testing and punishing schools and toward helping schools improve their capacity to serve all children well. We believe we are on this road at East Side by providing all students with different avenues of learning and more authentic and engaging ways of exhibiting their understanding of what they learn.

Philosophically, our school does not believe in state-mandated exams as the best measure of success. Rather, we believe that a well-constructed curriculum with high standards for all students and differentiated approaches to learning will prepare students for a variety of assessments, performance-based or test-based, and, more important, for success in college and beyond. Alfie Kohn states in *The Case against Standardized Tests* that the arguments for standardized tests are as follows:

1. They are an objective measure of achievement.
2. They improve accountability, or proof that schools are helping students learn.
3. They provide measured outcomes.

At East Side we believe "measurable outcomes [from standardized test] may be the least significant results of learning. . . . [S]tandardized tests punish the thinking test taker" (Kohn 4). We feel strongly about encouraging our students to be thinkers and to be able to exhibit their different habits of mind in performance-based assessments that are authentic and engage the students in their own learning process. We do not believe classroom time should be spent on prepping for tests but rather on "real learning" (Kohn 26). We believe that a student who is able to orally defend his or her understanding of curricular content in a roundtable presentation, or run a thirty-minute discussion on a sophisticated novel, or write a proposal letter to a film company explaining why a novel he or she read should be made into a movie, is held accountable for his or her own learning. The assessments are grounded in the curriculum we have developed to emphasize scholarly and real-world skills. The curriculum allows students to internalize, synthesize, and express skills to others. Authentic assessment is connected to both our high standards with literacy and our desire to promote "Accountable Talk," developed by Sarah Michaels and Catherine O'Connor through the Institute for Learning. This "sharpens students' thinking by reinforcing their ability to use and create knowledge" (*The Principles of Learning*, http://www.instituteforlearning.org). To convince adults of students' understanding of the content, authentic assessment requires that the students must have a deep level of understanding. Using these assessments signifies what we value at East Side—a value different than the standardized norm and a hope for change of that norm—because "assessment is a direct representation of what we value and how we assign that value" (Huot 8).

To create accountable assessments that are authentic and engaging, teachers at East Side use a type of backward curriculum planning modeled on the ideas promoted by Grant Wiggins and Jay McTighe in *Understanding by Design*. The concept of this type of curricular planning is to start with the big ideas and/or concepts that students should understand within a unit and spend time creating assessment tools that will allow teachers to measure students' understanding of those ideas. Basically, we want to think about where the students will be—what they will have learned and know—at the end of the unit, the year, and, ultimately, their time at East Side. In the context of our school, relevancy is key to both the development of curriculum and assessments. As Alfred Tatum promotes, we believe in an empowering curriculum that focuses on "engaging students with text and discussion about real issues they face . . . using meaningful literacy activities . . . [and] connecting the social, the economic, and the political to the educational" (Tatum 54). This is reflected in our unit plans and our assessments. Wiggins and McTighe define assessment as "the act of determining the extent to which curricular goals are being and have been achieved" (4). Assessments do not have to be alternative—they may include quizzes, essays, short-answer tests, reports—but there does need to be a variety of them and they do need to be authentic.

The focus of this book is on authentic assessment in English classrooms, assessments that can be adapted to other classroom environments. We provide a brief outline of the curriculum and highlight the assessment tools of three different teachers within the school who have extensive experience teaching sixth through twelfth grade. The first part gives an in-depth description of our independent reading program. Our independent reading program is rooted in the philosophies set forth by Richard Allington: (a) students need a protected time to read; (b) students must be able to choose books they love; and (c) they are immersed in a curriculum that cares about them (3–4). The independent reading program is a pillar of our school community and begins in sixth grade. Every student at East Side engages in thirty minutes of sustained silent reading every day in grades 6–10 and three days a week in grades 11–12. The independent reading program culminates with a project during the twelfth-grade year in which students must engage an adult in forty minutes of conversation about a novel they have both read. This project is an alternative assessment that allows the students to show their ownership over independent reading. We describe this assessment in great contextual detail, allowing teachers and administrators to see how it works in our school and that the project could be adapted in some form to another environment.

The second part of the book explains and provides the step-by-step process for roundtables and portfolio presentations at East Side. It is our belief that the roundtable is authentic because in the "assessment of performance we thereby learn whether students can intelligently use what they have learned in situations that increasingly approximate adult situations" (Wiggins 21). Roundtables are an end-of-semester and end-of-year assessment used in all classes at East Side Community High School. They are a highly valued assessment that often becomes a celebration of student work, knowledge, and skills. We detail the rationale at our school for using roundtables and the evolution of the portfolio process within the context of East Side, and suggest ways that different schools could include similar processes.

The third part focuses on developing a yearlong curriculum focused on social, political, and emotional relevancy to students' lives with a variety of alternative assessments during the same semester in which the students have to take a high-stakes exam. This part offers a step-by-step explanation of how to use *Understanding by Design* to generate alternative and authentic assessments for curricular units. We offer a side-by-side breakdown of the skills developed within the curriculum and the skills needed to succeed on the standardized test. This section also provides a detailed explanation of an end-of-year assessment that can be used as an alternative to the roundtable format that is outlined in Part 2. This assessment, a screenplay panel proposal presentation, focuses not only on the content of the curriculum but also on public speaking skills in a simulated professional environment. This part shows how assessments are designed to clearly allow students to exhibit their understanding of the goals set forth at the beginning of the unit, and should have some relevancy to real-world situations. Students should be able to do this during the unit, at the end of the unit, and at the culmination of the semester and year. As Wiggins and McTighe state, "a central premise of our argument is that understanding can be developed and evoked only through multiple methods of assessment" (4).

Each part of the book refers to handouts (available in the appendix) used by teachers and sample student work to add depth to the explanations. We have chosen to focus on independent reading, roundtables, and curricular design around assessment (including an alternative roundtable format) because these three elements have been crucial to the success of our students in terms of overall literacy, college entrance, and self-esteem.

1

Authentic Assessment of Independent Reading

A love of reading permeates the culture of East Side from sixth through twelfth grades. The principal's office is replete with a young adult literature library, and students often ask for permission to visit his office to browse for the latest titles. Independent reading, which provides students with the time to read silently and the choice to read whatever they want, is a core strategy East Side uses to improve literacy.

Every English class devotes significant time to independent reading, and each English classroom contains a library of titles for student borrowing. Research shows that one of the best ways to improve literacy is through sustained reading. The *New York Times* reported on a study by the National Endowment for the Arts that found that "students who read for fun nearly every day performed better on reading tests than those who reported reading never or hardly at all." The study goes on to explain "that reading appeared to correlate with academic achievement." Independent reading provides students with the books they want to read and time built into the school day to read. Students are expected to read at home as well.

East Side strives to create a true reading community, and not just within English classes. The principal runs a book club each month for which he supplies students with the selected text, and hosts a pizza lunch for students to discuss the book. By the time a student reaches twelfth grade at East Side, the hope is that he or she will have the literacy skills necessary to navigate college. The independent reading final project serves as a way for the school to celebrate the readers it has worked so hard to foster and also to assess the skills the students take with them when they leave high school.

1

In the Middle School Classroom

Includes Tips on Valuable Resources, Conferencing, and Reading Plans

Our Reading Crisis Seven Years Ago

Independent reading is not always an easy thirty minutes of reading with our students, who have varying reading issues and levels of interest in books. In 2002 we had almost a sense of hopelessness about the independent reading program. Many of us felt we could not make twenty students read when they didn't want to. We didn't know what to tell them to get them interested in books. We didn't know how to deal with their reading issues or even how to assess if they had a reading problem. The school had sufficient books of interest and a welcoming library, but having students just sit and read for thirty minutes made us wonder how effective that exercise was. What was happening in their brains as they read? What were we supposed to teach young adults about reading? What did they already know? How were we supposed to differentiate reading instruction and assess them on their individual levels?

We were trying to handle a reading crisis in both the middle and the high schools. Middle school students came to us with various skill levels, making differentiated instruction very difficult. Most students viewed reading as a chore and didn't know what "reading for pleasure" meant (Federman 12). Our students did not see literature as relevant to their lives. The average student "read" about four to six class novels or plays a year (Federman 12). Almost no students were reading at home as either required homework or for pleasure (Federman 12).

As we became better trained through countless professional development opportunities during the summer and school year, we became more skilled reading teachers. We came to understand that the one hour of reader's workshop that incorporated thirty minutes of quiet reading time in our middle school humanities classrooms was the base work for all the content reading the students would face in all of their other subjects. We noticed how students' reading levels determined how they took in the world around them and how deeply they could analyze their own existence in this world. The better we became at differentiating reading instruction to help students reach higher reading levels, the more we realized there was no better way to empower students than by giving them access to books and building reading time into their daily life routine. Students who can read at or close to grade level are ready to acquire knowledge, they are able to deepen their imaginations, they ask more thoughtful questions and can handle various viewpoints on one subject. An independent reader is defined by Kylene Beers in *When Kids Can't Read: What Teachers Can Do* as:

> those readers who are skilled at the cognitive and affective demands of reading and see the benefit in and derive pleasure from this skill. (p. 13)

Independent readers are not using their energy to get through words, and are not overwhelmed when they have to read more than a paragraph or come up with strategies to compensate for their reading inadequacies. In *Teaching Reading to Black Adolescent Males: Closing the Achievement Gap*, Alfred Tatum, who specializes in the literacy development of young African American men, states:

> First, increased reading achievement and literacy development among America's poor black males can provide them with greater opportunity to participate in all the good that America has to offer. It can also lead to higher levels of college enrollment, lower levels of unemployment, a reduction in violent crimes, and the lower incarceration rates of black men. (p. 15)

If our young people are not independent readers and cannot access many types of texts and negotiate various types of reading skills needed in their many subject areas, their chances of doing well in middle and high school are close to none. The only alternative to doing well in school is doing well in street life, which can lead to incarceration and death. In *To Be a Reader: Engaging Teen and Preteen Boys in Active Literacy*, William Brozo writes about how a strong literacy program can keep our reluctant male readers who don't thrive in school from becoming "nowhere kids":

> To presume that reading itself will transform conditions that plague young men, such as poverty, alcohol and drug abuse, crime and irresponsible fathering, is recklessly naïve; however, to ignore the potential of active literacy for ensuring that fewer adolescent males become nowhere kids is equally naïve. (p. 156)

Effective Resources for Reading Teachers

Eight million young people across the country, from fourth to twelfth grade, read below grade level (NCES, 2005). At East Side Community High School (ESCHS), every middle school humanities teacher has received training at the Teachers College Reading and Writing Project on how to build our students' stamina and comprehension through direct lessons that target skill development. It's almost impossible to state in words the impact the summer institutes at the Teachers College Reading and Writing Project has had on the collective teaching practices of the middle school teachers. Our success with teaching instruction and informal conferencing has been a direct result of our summer training and the visits made by project staff developers who come into our classrooms to help further illuminate how to transfer what we learned during the summer into each of our classrooms. As NYC public school teachers working in an inner-city school that faces the hardships of getting dependent readers to develop their reading skills quickly to try to close the achievement gap, we find great value in working with the Teachers College Reading and Writing Project.

Another reading program that helps teachers identify, monitor, and make individualized reading plans for each student in an efficient manner is the Developmental Reading Assessment (www.pearsonschool.com). It helps measure accuracy, fluency, and comprehension so that teachers can make reading plans that will most benefit the needs of each student.

Other useful resources we have used in our curriculum planning and assessment practices at ESCHS come from teacher reading circles. Besides going to conferences and workshops, the humanities teachers also read selected chapters of different pedagogical books to learn about the various theories and research that can deepen our practice. We have valued the suggestions of Richard L. Allington in *What Really Matters for Struggling Readers,* in which he outlines how to respond to the differentiated needs of struggling readers in a teacher-friendly manner. Our staff also values the ideas of Ellen Keens in *To Understand,* which guides teachers to make more accurate decisions about their reading curriculum by helping students engage more deeply with texts. Also, *When Kids Can't Read: What Teachers Can Do* by Kylene Beers has been instrumental in giving us practical strategies during individualized reading conferences and helping us make better curriculum decisions throughout the year for our struggling readers.

You will often find that young adults who are good readers are powerful human beings because they have access to learning beyond the classroom, can read meaningful text about issues that affect them, and have a better chance of overcoming academic and social barriers. Quick, trustworthy, and varied reading assessments become key in helping students develop their reading skills.

Reading Assessments and the Importance of Gathering Other Reading Data

In properly assessing a student's reading level, it's important to use various forms of data because the variety can gauge the reading skills and habits more authentically. Also, assessment shouldn't take too much time or else teachers will be reluctant to assess students on a routine basis.

The general routine of how we assess and make plans for our readers at ESCHS follows the path below. The days in which each item happens varies for each teacher, but we have included a suggested time line:

One to two days: Observe students' reading habits.

One to two days: Use a word examiner to estimate their reading level. We do our best to match students with books that correspond with their predicted reading level . No one should be given a book that is too difficult for them.

One to two weeks: Complete a more in-depth standardized reading assessment.

One to two weeks: Have an individualized reading conference with each student, starting with the readers who noticeably struggle with their book.

One to two weeks: After each reading conference, create a reading plan that best speaks to the differentiated needs of the reader.

These steps can take up to a month to complete, but this time is crucial as it helps us target, research, and plan for the reading needs of each student in an efficient yet accurate manner. Now that we have a general overview, we will further discuss strategies for each step on this time line for assessing our readers.

On the first day, when we observe our students as they read, we can gather very helpful information about them while they authentically try to read their book. Independent readers have many outward qualities that can be observed while they read. Most independent readers:

- Settle into their book quickly
- Focus their eyes on the page for long periods of time
- Hold their book firmly and often turn the page in two to three minutes
- Don't get distracted with small movements around them
- Furrow their brows when reading
- Have emotional reactions like laughing, being surprised, or being upset by certain parts of the book
- Read silently without moving their lips

Dependent readers tend to lose their focus very easily, need many reading breaks, drop their book often, and wiggle in their seat, wondering aloud how much time is left for reading.

Based on outward, easily observable reading habits, we prioritize students who are not actively reading and assess them using a more standardized method during the next two weeks of class. Some teachers prioritize their struggling readers first by immediately having their conferences and reading plans completed before getting to the rest of the class. This strategy is acceptable when we have too many students in a class, when we feel overwhelmed by new assessment procedures, or when we simply want to help motivate reluctant readers. But it is important to try our best to assess the reading needs of all of our students because even the capable readers deserve differentiated instruction to make them extraordinary and give them the best chance of success.

The next step is to get a rough idea of every student's reading level and make sure that for the next few weeks they are choosing books they can read with relative ease. Completing a formal reading assessment takes about fifteen minutes per student, and it can take many weeks to assess an entire class. Therefore, knowing how quickly a student can decode words is a quick way to roughly gauge what level they can read. However, it does not give us the data on fluency and comprehension that a more formal reading assessment can.

Teachers at ESCHS use a word examiner list, which lists words by grade level, from the qualitative reading inventory packet. For each grade level, there is a list of twenty words that a reader should be able to decode quickly. The student copy simply shows a list of words in columns. The teacher copy has the words labeled by grade level. This is done so that when we administer the word examiner, students are not self-conscious about their performance. We usually start the word examiner list assessment by saying, "Sorry to interrupt your reading, but today I wanted to see how well you can take words apart when reading. There may be some really hard words on the page, and I don't expect you to know all of them. I'm just looking to see what you do when you see a hard word and how you try to say it out loud. This is to help me know you better as a reader."

As long as the assessment is done quickly and privately, most students don't mind reading a group of random words on a page and will show us outwardly what they do when they see a hard word. We can gather information about their understanding of phonics and syllables, and about their confidence in applying previously learned strategies. We can estimate students' decoding levels once they get three or more words wrong on the word examiner list, or if they struggle more than necessary with the list. We spend about three to five minutes per student with the word examiner list, and after two days we have a rough idea of which students do not have the appropriate decoding skills for their age level and need to be supported immediately.

We share all our data with the learning specialist, who may choose to visit during reading time and help those who struggle with decoding to find appropriate books, or pull them out of class and read aloud to them to ensure that independent reading is pleasurable from the beginning of the school year.

Once we have an idea of the students' decoding levels, we look to see what books are being read during independent reading and make sure each student is matched with an appropriate book that will not frustrate them. As we gather data about our students, it's also important to share the data with the rest of the teachers in that grade level so that they too can plan their curriculum in ways that support developing reading habits and decrease the chances of frustrating the struggling students.

After getting an idea of each student's reading level and matching students to books that will most likely work for them, we complete a more in-depth standardized reading assessment. The one we use in the middle school is the Teachers College Fiction Reading Level Assessment. This packet offers a set of informal reading selections for narrative texts that correlates to the Fountas and Pinnell system for leveling books (http://rwproject.tc.columbia.edu). This assessment takes about fifteen to twenty minutes per student and can help identify which level of texts students can read independently, allowing students to practice all the reading strategies they are learning during reading workshop (http://rwproject.tc.columbia.edu). The assessment provides an analysis of comprehension, miscues, and fluency from levels J–Z (http://rwproject.tc.columbia.edu).

When we assess students' reading,we do so by observing them and taking notes over a few days. We then use the word examiner and the Teachers College Fiction Reading Level Assessment packet. We also review all other data gathered from previous teachers and school records. By getting various forms of data, we feel confident that we understand the students' reading habits, decoding skills, and comprehension skills, all of which empowers us to help him or her in an organic way and create a reading plan that lends itself to the fastest results. We also are better equipped to tailor reading conferences more individually to help each student with his or her specific needs.

For the incoming sixth graders, once their school records are sent over, teachers can look at individual records to see what their incoming students' reading levels were in fifth grade and the results of the fourth-grade ELA exam. Even though city and statewide reading tests have limited data on the reading capabilities our students have as learners, all of the information gathered about them as readers can be revealing to an extent. We always need to be informed about our students with quality reading data that can help serve them. It should never be left to one teacher or administrator to look over records or collect these data. These kinds of tasks are difficult and should be done as a community of teachers and administrators.

Once we assess our students' reading levels and chart the gathered data, it becomes easier to identify whether a student suffers from stagnant reading skills. If we feel that a student's reading gap is increasing in our classroom, we own that problem in the same way a lifeguard owns the problem when they see someone drowning. This is our "red flag, do not pass go, pull all the alarms, call a national emergency, and handle this situation immediately" case!

As educators, we all need to know that when a student's reading level is stagnant, even after various teacher interventions and thoughtful teaching, it is appropriate to bring in a team of others to help us brainstorm solutions to a child's particular reading issue. It does not mean we are not good teachers or that the level of instruction in our class is not effective. We are not only educators with the responsibility of getting our students to be powerful readers, but we are also their advocates. We must put aside our own inter-school politics and issues between teachers and administrators to champion for the reading lives of our students. Advocating for our students and helping resolve their educational needs as a team is vital to solving the reading crisis and learning gap that is affecting our inner-city youth.

Sexy Libraries!

In getting students to want to look for books they will love to read, the teachers make sure their libraries are attractive and stand out in the classroom. Each classroom has about seven to ten fairly new and matching bookshelves that reach the students' eye level. Colorful plastic bins are clearly labeled to help students identify the genres available. The labels on each bin are large and can be seen from afar. We do this intentionally because we hope that as students see the different genres and themes available to them, they will be more willing to try out the different bins. Listed are the most common bin labels that help create a fun library that gets students curious about books:

Gender Specific

- Teen Boys
- Teen Girls

Humor

- Comics
- Funny Books
- Graphic Novels

Highlighted Authors

- Matt Christopher
- Gary Paulsen
- Judy Blume

Poetry

- Creative Voices

Genres of Interest

- Diaries
- Mystery
- Aliens
- Fantasy
- Gross, Disgusting, and Rude
- Cool People—Biographies
- Action
- Quick Reads
- Science on My Mind
- Books That Fit into My Pocket

Political/Race Issues

- Latino Characters
- Politics
- African American Characters
- World Issues

Series

- Spiderwick
- Harry Potter
- Blueford Series
- Orca Soundings Series

Health and Dating Issues

- I'm Not a Kid Anymore
- Gay / Lesbian / Bisexual / Questioning / Transgender

Oftentimes, students gravitate toward themes and genres they know the most about. But as their reading tastes develops, we hope to introduce them to new genres. Therefore, we make sure that even from their seats they are able to see the different labeled bins and consider previewing the books when it's their time to use the library.

The choice of books to place in one's in-class library is extremely important. At the beginning of the school year, we place easier books in the bins. We make sure there are many series in various genres and lots of graphic novels, funny books, poetry, and urban fiction that are quick reads for reluctant readers. We want to ensure that any book a student chooses will be close to their reading level. At ESCHS, we've also committed to leveling each book using the Fountas and Pinnell leveling chart that can be found online. We do not organize the bins by reading level, because each student is not a level. Each student has interests and concerns and wants authentic reading experiences that match their life experiences. To get them to read, the labels on each reading bin need to reflect the multitude of interests our students have.

Because it's important that each student comprehend his or her books and can make meaning of them, each book is leveled yet organized by topic or genre. During the first week of school, some sixth-grade students know their reading levels because their elementary schools also use the Fountas and Pinnell leveling charts. These students usually find books that interest them and can better gauge what books in each bin work for them, using the leveling on the back cover as a navigation tool. However, the students who are not aware of their reading level need to know that most books in the library are accessible to them. Therefore, we usually start the library in September with easier books that range from Level M (second-grade level) to Level U (mid-sixth-grade level).

Of course, as the year goes on, each month we introduce more challenging books to the in-class library. We make students aware of the new books being placed in the bins by doing quick book talks to the class or recommending books to individual students who will benefit from reading them due to their subject matter. Also, some of the more organized teachers have a reserve of books in their closet to use during reading conferences when they make reading plans. These are books set aside for students with high reading levels that range from Level V to Level Z. We introduce these books to them more privately in the beginning of the school year because we know they can handle starting their reading plans on a higher level and can finish the books within a week.

At the beginning of the school year, it's important for students to choose easier books because they will finish them faster and develop stamina for words on a page. Their hunger for reading also will increase, which prompts them to want to recommend books to one another. It's important that readers feel good about reading from the beginning and know that they are capable of completing a book within a few days to a week. Some of the students tell us at the end of the first week of school that this is their first time ever finishing a book without feeling the need to abandon it halfway through. They feel proud of themselves and hold that confidence with them when they start reading more challenging books a few weeks later.

Teachers and administrators often ask us how we can afford to buy all the books that fill our individual classroom libraries. The principal, Mark Federman, has explained that instead of spending money on textbooks that students hate to read, he gives each teacher that amount of money to buy students real books they will be enthusiastic about reading. For example, a student edition Holt Environmental Science textbook costs $71.45, according to Federman. If a science teacher has 140 students divided among five periods of the school day, in total the school has to spend $10,003 on textbooks. At ESCHS, we choose to buy one class set of textbooks that would cost approximately $1,995. That would leave $8,008 left for independent reading books. Our school gets the same money as every other school, and budget cuts affect us in the same ways. Therefore, we use the majority of our school funding that is set aside for textbooks to purchase real books that students will love to read. We've also purchased discounted books from used bookstores in New York City, and have received deep discounts plus delivery of books to each classroom from Booksource.com.

Our reading instruction will only matter to students when they desire certain books that are still too difficult for them. There needs to be a buzz about certain books in the reading community that includes the sixth-, seventh-, and eighth-grade reading selections. Students will want to experience the reading instruction taught through mini-lessons and work on their reading plans so they can access more sophisticated texts.

Assessing Students through Differentiated Reading Conferences

The reading conference provides a time and space for differentiated instruction based on the natural abilities of each student. Once we are more familiar with their skills and abilities, we schedule independent reading for forty-five minutes on the days of the week that we are not doing direct whole-class reading lessons and/or read-alouds. This gives us time to create small conferring groups for ten to fifteen minutes at a time so that the students can practice their skills with us and in front of each other. The conferring groups help students see the variety of thinking patterns other readers use to achieve the same skill. It also helps teachers meet with more students in a short period of time, while giving the small group direct attention to their reading gaps. We avoid forcing everyone to try their developing skills in the same way and acknowledge that there are several thinking patterns readers naturally use that can help them to understand texts deeply.

Individualized reading conferences provide students with more tailored reading instruction. During individual reading conferences, we already have an idea of what reading issue is preventing the student from developing further. We get this information from the data collection done through classroom observations of their reading, the word examiner, the in-depth reading assessment, and the collection of reading scores from their elementary school and classroom observations. Our individual reading conferences need to be planned and last no longer than fifteen minutes. When conferences go on too long, the student gets tired and the teacher finds meeting with so many students an exhausting task. We prepare beforehand by deciding what set of skills the student needs to learn in the next few weeks to get to the next reading level. Leona Gross, a teacher at ESCHS, has created the reading conference prep sheet that incorporates the ideas of Teachers College in understanding the natural progression of skill development from one reading level to the next (Handout 1.1; all handouts are in the appendix). We will either use a text from a read-aloud previously done in the classroom or use the student's independent reading book to model how powerful readers think about their book. We might tailor specific note-taking tips in the reader's notebook or on a sticky note for the next few weeks to help students practice the skills they need to move into the next reading level. We can see students become better readers as they speak and write with more sophistication about their independent reading book and in classroom read-alouds. Our evidence that students are becoming better readers comes from checking in on their notebook work that we have tailored to their needs. We also listen to how they discuss their book with us during reading conferences and with their partner in the classroom. We also should be able to observe focused readers who seem drawn into their books during independent reading time on a regular basis.

Once we can see some development in the students' reading, it is important to reevaluate their reading skills after two or three months. Rather than holding another individual conference, we test each student using more in-depth assessment that can take fifteen to twenty minutes. We have the students read a text that is one level higher than the reading level they were on a few months ago. If they can successfully read and comprehend the text, we know they are becoming better readers.

Students who have large reading gaps (i.e., between grade level and their reading level) but who love the books recommended to them and read daily improve their skills rather quickly. In a few months they can make significant progress because the skills they need to practice are very tangible. Our more sophisticated readers usually see improvement in six months or more because the skills they need to develop often require higher-level thinking and take more time to fully attain.

In addition to having conferences around skill development, there is also a need for conferences related to the meaning derived from certain book choices. The reading community cannot be solely skill-driven to improve their reading levels. It's paramount that the reading experience lead middle school students into a self-reflective journey. The students must first be able to see the impact books can have on their lives. Therefore, another type of powerful conferencing based on student assessment and knowledge of their interests is having conversations around how students are relating to a book on a personal level. If they have no personal connection to the book, students may be reading something that is too difficult for them, or perhaps they don't know what may interest them. Often the reluctant readers are male students who think they are too tough and manly to be reading. They associate reading with either female activities or highly academic activities that they cannot connect with. Yet it is often these same students who tell us anecdotes about being approached by gang members who are either their neighbors or family members and tempted into street life.

This handful of male middle school students who dislike reading are often asked and consider taking a role in street life. The NYC street life of having a gang family, having opportunities to make money through the selling of "soft drugs" such as marijuana, and hanging with a manly looking crew of other young men who will "have their back" when their own families may not be there for them is often a more attractive option than the rigor of school life, which includes independent reading and listening to mini-lessons. These adolescents feel valued when local gang members recognize them and give them scarves or beads as "gifts" to wear in support of the gang.

As teachers, our reading conferences also need to address these issues and give our students knowledge through books that can help them transform their lives. The conferencing can be a way to discuss issues our young people are facing outside the school building that may be difficult for them to bring up and get an honest response to during other times of the school day. It is much easier to discuss the main character Tookie in the book *Life in Prison* and the decisions he is making than to directly discuss that individual student's life. Alfred Tatum discusses the role meaningful reading instruction has on African American males. In *Teaching Reading to Black Adolescent Males: Closing the Achievement Gap*, he writes:

> When teachers give their black male students skills and strategies without showing them the transformative possibilities associated with those skills and strategies, the students will find them to be useless tools. This is what happens, for example, when teachers use test prep in an attempt to improve students' reading scores. Many students in class, not just black males, are likely to ask the question, "Why are we doing this?" They may also complain, "We did this already." If teachers are unable to make the skills and strategies they teach relate in some way to their students' lives, the students will not see the need to use the skills and strategies. (85)

We can argue that Tatum's focus on creating meaningful instruction can have deep implications for African American males, but his advice also makes sense for educators trying to develop a healthy reading community made up of all races.

Reading Plans

As reading teachers, we are expected to create reading plans to push our students forward and to check in on their plans often. From October to March, each student should have completed at least two reading plans that have been created from information gleaned through conferring with students about their books, looking over the notes they take about their books, reflecting about their reading logs, observing how they read in class, and being plugged into their life outside of school.

A reading plan uses the assessment results from repeated classroom observations during independent reading, informal conferences with individual students about their reading interests, and the results from the fiction reading level assessments. It's important to make a reading plan that encompasses results from various sources to make sure it constitutes a holistic reading approach. The reading plan should make students feel empowered because we have listened to them while helping them move forward with their reading life. It should be a feasible plan that gets students motivated to improve their reading skills in a couple of months.

Various types of reading plans can help build different skills. As we get to know our students better, we can tailor each reading plan to improve their skills and to fit reading into their home life. It's important to highlight specific skill work that students need to practice to move on to the next reading level. The following is an example of options our literacy coach, Elisa Zonana, has collected for our use:

Habit:

- Reading every night at home for ___ minutes; reading on Sundays
- Reading fifty pages each night at home
- Reading three more pages each day in class (from, say, about 22 pages to about 25 pages)
- Reread a book or series paying attention to ________
- Form a book club or partnership

Skill/Strategy:

Focus on . . .

- Predicting, envisioning, interpreting, inferring

Genre:

Try a new genre like . . .

- Fantasy, mystery, historical fiction, classics, nonfiction about ________

Fluency:

- Practice making the tone match the characters' emotions
- Make dialogue sound like talking
- Pause by paying attention to punctuation
- Read dramatically

Reading plans can be created for a one-month period. Most plans range between one week and one month, with several teacher check-ins. First, and most important, decide for each student which habit or skill they will improve or try. The reading plan needs to clearly highlight which books they will read and by what date they should finish each book. Also, decide what work needs to be done in the reader's notebook to support reading comprehension and skill development.

At ESCHS we are fortunate to have amazing leadership that is committed to keeping our class sizes down to eighteen students per class in the middle school. But in many schools across the nation, having twenty-five to thirty students in each classroom may be more typical. Completing a reading plan for every student may seem difficult to accomplish while also getting the routines of independent reading going and doing instruction during reader's workshop. Every child requires at least two reading plans a semester to feel committed to meeting valuable goals. We give priority to making reading plans for students by their reading level and for those whom we observe as being reluctant readers, regardless of their reading level. We want to make sure they are motivated to read and have books they love. The next group we focus on includes the students with low reading levels and gaps in their reading skill development. In sixth grade, this means students in Levels J through R (from second-grade level to lower fifth-grade level). We typically meet last with students who are on grade level or above. With these students it is important to highlight a variety of genres and authors they might not yet have been exposed to. The more genres they learn to negotiate, the more powerful they can be in school. As part of these students' plan, we work on skills that push them into the next grade level. Typically, high-level readers can take six months to a year to show substantial skill improvement because they are practicing their skills on various genres and engaging in higher-level thinking work that takes time to solidify. For these students, completing one book a week, applying higher-level critical thinking skills to the books they are reading, and having several opportunities to discuss their reading with peers who are doing similar readings are all crucial to their success.

Empowering Families with Reading Data

An important step in advocating for our students' reading needs is sharing the assessments results with students' families on a consistent basis. Principal Mark Federman offers a presentation titled *Ten Ways That Parents/Families Can Help Their Children Become Better Readers* for several days at the beginning of the school year that helps explain to family members how to use the reading report to help their child with reading at home.

A simple handout distributed during the *Ten Ways That Parents/Families Can Help Their Children Become Better Readers* presentation makes simple suggestions for how parents can better support their child's reading life outside of school (Handout 1.2). The message ESCHS sends to all parents and caregivers is that they are part of the team that will make their child successful, and that we have expectations of them to make reading a priority at home.

Once the goal of making each student a powerful reader becomes a school-wide initiative that parents have also bought into, humanities teachers make sure to complete a reading report for each student that is to be shared with family members twice a year alongside report card grades. Every full-time teacher in each content area of our school is also an advisor who is responsible for communicating with family members on a consistent basis about the progress of each student in his or her class. When family members attend report card meetings, the advisors review the reading report with them. They read the document with the family member to ensure all parts are understood and that the family knows the student's reading level. We encourage and empower parents by giving them vital information about reading levels, current reading goals, and a suggested plan of action for reading outside the classroom.

2

Authentic Assessment of Independent Reading as a Graduation Requirement

Before sending students to college or into the workforce, we hope that our commitment to reading during the students' senior year has nurtured literate adults ready to parse the world for meaning. The independent reading final project aims to provide an experience for students to demonstrate their growth into literate, articulate, and persuasive adults. The beauty of this project lies in its ability to transmit the skills and messages of our school's reading culture in one unit.

"East Side is obsessed with making sure that you are a reader," we tell the twelfth graders in mid-May. They nod their heads knowingly. They have been spending time in school and at home reading independently since the sixth grade. A quick glance at our well-stocked classroom library reveals how seriously this school has committed to nurturing the love of reading. Students look over their independent reading records from the past years and begin to tally the number of books they have read over the course of their careers at East Side. The numbers can be staggering.

The independent reading final project occurs at the end of senior year. To complete the project, each East Side student conducts an analytical discussion on a work of literature with an adult who has read the same book. The students choose their book from eight options and work in a group to read and analyze their chosen text in preparation for their discussion. Students select one book from among the following choices:

- *Breath, Eyes, Memory*, Edwidge Danticat
- *A Lesson Before Dying*, Ernest J. Gaines
- *The Curious Incident of the Dog in the Night-Time*, Mark Haddon
- *Beasts of No Nation*, Uzodinma Iweala
- *The Secret Life of Bees*, Sue Monk Kidd

- *Foxfire: Confessions of a Girl Gang*, Joyce Carol Oates
- *Catcher in the Rye*, J. D. Salinger
- *The Kite Runner*, Khaled Hosseini

All eight books deal with the theme of growing up and characters' struggles to find their place in the world. This theme feels fitting for students on the cusp of graduation. However, just about any text would work for this project as long as you can find adults who are familiar with the novel or who are willing to read it.

The students are responsible for coming prepared to the conversation with an analysis of significant passages, discussion questions, and an interpretation of the author's purpose. On the first day of the unit, students are given a handout (see page 21) that lays out the expectations for the assessment.

Each student meets individually with an adult evaluator. The adult may be an East Side teacher or a member of the community. The role of the adult is to engage with the student in a discussion of the book, much as one would with peers in a book club, classmates in a college seminar, or even with a friend over coffee. It is the student's responsibility to run the conversation. At the end of the conversation, the adult completes a rubric (p. 22) and offers brief feedback to the student. Sixty percent of the students' unit grade is based on the rubric. The rubric offers specific instructions on how the evaluator should grade the conversation, clearly explaining what constitutes the labels excellent, good, fair, and needs improvement. We give the adult reader this rubric at the beginning of the project to emphasize the importance of this assessment. The rubric is detailed in an attempt to improve inter-rater reliability. Because some guests may not be teachers, we hope that explicit guidelines will add meaning to the assessment. While the conversation is occurring, the teachers are not present. Discussions are often scheduled during class time, so we must rely on the judgment of the evaluator.

Structures to Scaffold Success

Students spend three weeks preparing for their final discussion. The emphasis on student agency is central to the success of this project. When students feel ownership over their book, they become far more invested in the project and more animated in their discussions. Students must be given a choice of texts, and we offer the students a selection of books reflecting a wide range of skill levels. Some of the books appeal more directly to male students and others to female students. The list of authors is racially and geographically diverse.

Independent Reading Final Project

The goal of this project is for you to demonstrate your proficiency in comprehending, analyzing, questioning, and discussing a work of literature. You will run an analytical discussion with an adult member of the community who is familiar with your book.

What you must prepare for your final project:

a. **Three passages from the novel that struck you**

For each passage you must be prepared to explain:

- An explanation of why you selected that passage
- What the passage reveals about the characters, the setting, the conflicts, or the author's purpose
- What questions the passage raises about any of the above

b. **Five discussion questions**

- You must have notes on your opinions on possible answers for each question.

c. **Author's purpose**

Write one paragraph on what you think the author's purpose was in writing this book. What does he or she want the reader to take away from reading the book? Do you think the author succeeds?

East Side Community High School Independent Reading Final Project Rubric

Student________________ Book_______________ Evaluator__________________

	Excellent	Good	Fair	Needs Improvement
Analysis	Sophisticated analysis, demonstrating in-depth understanding of selected passages and the characters and themes in the text	Presents a thoughtful understanding of passage's significance with some in-depth analysis	Presents a basic understanding of selected passages with limited analysis	Shows limited understanding of passage's significance
Discussion Questions	Questions got to key themes, were thoughtful, and pushed analysis deeper	Questions were open-ended and prompted discussion but did not always lead to deeper analysis	Questions prompted some discussion	Questions were basic and the student's opinions poorly developed
Evidence	Student was able to support all opinions with relevant evidence	Student was able to support most opinions with relevant evidence	Student had a limited ability to support ideas with evidence	Student was unable to support ideas with evidence
Author's Purpose	Student had a deep understanding of author's purpose	Student presented a well-thought-out understanding of author's purpose	Student had some sense of author's purpose	Student lacked a clear sense of author's purpose
Familiarity	Student knew the book backwards and forwards	Student is very familiar with characters, themes, and key events	Student struggled to remember certain characters, themes, and events	Student was unable to recall significant characters, themes, events
Presentation	Student started the conversation with ease. Student was extremely well prepared and did not read from notes. Made eye contact.	Started the conversation with ease. Student was well prepared but sometimes relied on notes.	Student's poise faltered at times. Student had difficulty beginning the conversation. Student was prepared.	Student lacked poise. Student was unable to begin the discussion. Student lacked preparation.

To generate excitement for the project and the books, we bring in guest teachers who love the opportunity to pitch their favorite text. Each teacher presents a brief synopsis and reasons why he or she loves that particular book. Mark Federman, the school's principal, excitedly stops by each class to tell students how he had discovered *Catcher in the Rye* as an angst-ridden teenager and the impact it had on his life. He also touts it as a staple of the American literary canon.

Andrea, the librarian, reads the first few lines of *The Curious Incident of the Dog in the Night-Time* and tells students, "You have probably never read a book with a narrator like Christopher. His insights into the world will keep you reading." These guests radiate a love of reading and remind the students from the first day of this project that they are part of a community of readers and that people care deeply about their insights into literature.

After hearing each pitch, students then rank their choices and we put together a group of three to five students for each book. In some cases, two groups may read the same book in a class. Students have up to two days to switch texts. One group of students grew frustrated after their second day with Holden's emphasis on phonies. They had all given *Catcher in the Rye* a shot, and as a group decided to switch to *Beasts of No Nation*. The one student who had found Holden amusing rather than grating chose to hold on to his copy to read for extra credit. The chance to switch books gives students enough time to realize if they have chosen a book that is too difficult, or one that simply does not interest them.

As a group, students create a reading calendar and divide their text into nightly homework assignments. Though students dictate their reading schedule, nightly homework is still given. We rely heavily on sticky notes. Whenever students read a passage that strikes them as significant to the plot, a character's development, imagery, or symbolism, they mark it and briefly explain why they have selected that passage.

Students are given some time in class to read most days. Each day, students are responsible for running their own discussions within their groups. They share sticky notes and push each other to understand and analyze. Having students run their own discussions, talking about what actually matters to them in the text, is excellent preparation for the final project and also for the type of independent work they will be expected to do in college.

Students are aware from the first day of the project that they will need to explain three significant passages, pose five discussion questions, and present an interpretation of the author's purpose for the final discussion (see homework assignment in box). They read with these three tasks in mind, recognizing that the notes they take will become the backbone of their final discussion.

Teacher-driven lessons are a component of the preparation. Students are asked to explore the role of gender in their works, notice what literary devices the author employs, and write an advice letter to the protagonist. We do this to push our students' ability to analyze texts.

IR Final Project Homework

A. Read up to the page your group has decided.

B. Each night you must select a passage you believe is significant and write a one-page analysis of that passage. (BE SURE TO MARK THE PAGE WITH A STICKY NOTE)

C. Discussion

Each day your group will discuss the reading. One student will be assigned to prepare five discussion questions on the reading. One student must take notes on what the group discusses. Both discussion questions and notes will be collected every day.

D. There will be periodic QUIZZES.

To encourage the use of literary vocabulary in the final discussion, students refresh their memories of key terms and connect them to their novel using the following prompt:

Using Sophisticated Literary Language in Your Discussion

Terms to Define:
Linear Narrative:
Nonlinear Narrative:
First-Person Narrative:
Third-Person Omniscient Narrative:
Third-Person Limited:
Mood:

1. Is the narrative linear or nonlinear? If it's nonlinear, in what ways? WHY might the author have made the choice that he or she did?
2. Is the novel first person, third limited, or third omniscient? Why might the author have made that choice?
3. What is the mood of the novel? Defend your answer.
4. List three themes in your novel.
5. List two symbols and explain what you think they mean.

The Power of Modeling

In addition to the lessons designed to push analysis, the crucial teacher-driven element of this unit is modeling. This project is the first time students are asked to perform in this manner, so modeling elevates their confidence and the quality of their own work. Last year, immediately before beginning this unit, the whole class read *One Flew Over the Cuckoo's Nest* by Ken Kesey. We used this text as a model, pretending it was our book for the final project. We modeled each step of the project as students prepared. On the first day that students were assigned reading, we showed them examples demonstrating how we completed nightly notes on sticky notes. Over the course of the project, we showed them how we selected significant passages, created thought-provoking discussion questions, and interpreted the author's purpose (see Handouts 2.1 and 2.2).

In the days before students begin conducting their own discussions, we model this final, and least familiar, aspect of the assessment. Another English teacher is solicited to play the role of adult evaluator while the classroom teacher assumes the role of the nervous high school senior. Once again we use a text that all the students have read for this exercise. Students complete the rubric to assess the performance, and afterward we debrief what they have observed, give suggestions, and discuss alternatives. Since students are filling out the very same rubric with which they will be assessed, this serves as a way for them to familiarize themselves with the rubric to determine the standards to which they will be held.

The Analytical Discussion

Each student is paired with a teacher or a guest from the community who has read the same book as that student. To solicit evaluators, we email every East Side teacher and administrator, former East Side teachers, members of the school's partner organizations, and friends of teachers who love books (Example 2.1). *Catcher in the Rye* is a book people remember from their own school days. *The Secret Life of Bees* has been a commercial hit, so many people have read it. The narrator of *The Curious Incident of the Dog in the Night-Time* is an autistic boy who loves math, and the book has been widely read among teachers in the math department. Several teachers volunteered to read the lesser-known works such as *Foxfire* and *Beasts of No Nation*. The staff has rallied around this project, and the principal urges every English and history teacher to commit to at least two conversations. Many other teachers and administrators do multiple conversations as well. Outside guests generally meet with one student. We send each pair to either an empty classroom or the back of the library. Each conversation lasts between thirty and forty minutes.

The adult evaluators are instructed to exchange pleasantries but allow the student to begin the conversation. This is key, as we do not want students to rely on the benevolence of their evaluator but rather assert their confidence and preparation and steer the discussion.

On the back of the rubric, the adult takes notes on the conversation and then completes the rubric, giving the student both positive and negative feedback. Students are encouraged to come well prepared to their discussion with comprehensive notes. Example 2.2 in the appendix features Jeremiah's preparatory notes on *A Lesson Before Dying*. He met with Sayeeda, a former English teacher who had taught the book. The notes she took of their conversation are in Example 2.3 in the appendix.

Project Pitfalls

Logistics present the biggest challenge to the successful execution of this project. There are only seventy-five students in a senior class at East Side, but the pairing of each student with an adult who also has read the book remains a challenge. Books that are neither the staples of school curricula nor bestsellers present the biggest scheduling obstacles. However, many people express excitement about this project and agree to read a new book to participate. It is also taxing to coordinate the schedules of the evaluator and the student.

We try to schedule discussions at times when the students have English or lunch or immediately after school. Lunch is often appealing for outside guests who come to school during their lunch hour. Although ideally we want to have the student alone with an adult to keep each student responsible and on the spot, students can be paired so that two students who have read the book can meet with one adult. This can be beneficial, as the students can bounce ideas off each other, enriching the discussion. Other options for accommodating guests include having students go directly to the volunteer's place of employment or a convenient coffee shop. Other ideas would be to reach out to a local college professor to connect students with English majors or education majors.

Rationale

The structure of this project aims to mimic college English classes in which students are often expected to read a whole book before arriving at class and must be prepared to offer their ideas on the meaning of the text. However, the project contains built-in structures for added support to enable success—namely, students do not analyze the text entirely on their own, but rather work in small groups to tackle their chosen novel. They are evaluated independently but have the support of their peers during the process of preparing for the final discussion.

The primary aim of this project is to give students the opportunity to demonstrate their proficiency in comprehending, analyzing, questioning, and discussing a work of literature. These are all skills they have strengthened through years of independent reading at East Side. This project functions as a transition away from the primary style of reading literature in a high school classroom, in which whole-class novels are divided into nightly sections and students are asked guiding questions to aid their comprehension and foster analysis.

In *College Knowledge,* David Conley examines the skills he believes students must leave high school with to succeed in college. He emphasizes the creation of projects at the end of senior year.

> These culminating projects or demonstrations integrate the content knowledge expected of students who are prepared to enter college with the thinking, skills, and habits of mind that will be required of them shortly. The projects also require the personal characteristics, such as independent work, initiative, sustained effort, inquisitiveness, and attention to detail and quality, that will serve students well in the postsecondary environment. (76)

This project aspires to meet this suggestion, asking students to apply in an independent manner all the skills they have learned in their years at East Side.

The project assesses students' ability to speak about literature, so, in this sense, the project is twofold. Students must first read and analyze the text and then lead the discussion to clearly express their analysis. Discussion is a huge part of life in the English classroom, but rarely is the discussion part of assessment. Class participation is always factored into final grades, but the vast majority of our formal assessments are written. Generally, assessments demand that students respond to literature in the form of analytical essays and exams. The lack of assessments designed to challenge students to express their ideas orally means that too often the way a student's class participation grade is calculated is based on the frequency with which that student talks and not necessarily on his or her depth of understanding.

In this project, students are asked to submit the notes they used to prepare for their discussions, but they are not graded on their written work. Preparing students for accountable talk aids their confidence in discussing their ideas and backing them up with evidence.

As with so many of the assessments at East Side, this project is designed to imbue in students the belief that both their learning and their ability to discuss what they think matters. At the end of senior year, it is important to jolt a sense of urgency into the learning of our students.

It has been exciting to work with students and the school community on the development of this project. Former teachers love reconnecting with their students on an intellectual level. People who do not work in education but love reading have reported their sense of excitement about discussing a work of literature with a student. People who have loved the same book can develop a very special bond.

Students feel a tremendous amount of ownership over their selected novel and the discussion. Again, although Alfred Tatum focuses his analysis on the reading habits of black male students, his insights can be applied to many of our students. He cautions, "Teachers' failure to provide instruction that leads black males to read about, write about, and think about important issues related to their existence contributes to their invisibility and demasculinization in school and society" (49). Many of the discussions take on a celebratory air as the student reveals the depth of his or her understanding. Students relish the feeling of being an intellectual peer with an adult. This feeling is one we hope they take with them to college and beyond.

This experience reinforces and celebrates the independent reading culture we have worked so hard to establish. Beginning in the sixth grade, students are encouraged to embrace reading as a passion, a skill set, and, more important, a means to becoming a literate citizen able to read the world around them to effect change.

2

Roundtables and Other Performance-Based Assessments

At the end of each semester, rather than use the week devoted to standardized tests by the New York Department of Education for Regents exams, East Side hosts roundtables. The hallways are silent. But peeking into any classroom with a roundtable in session, a guest will see six or seven intellectual discussions happening simultaneously throughout the room. Groups of students, each with an adult facilitator, pore over the work from the semester as students explain their learning and growth. Students are focused, and at times nervous, to demonstrate what they have learned. Over the course of this week, every high school student will participate in a ninety-minute roundtable for each of his or her core subjects: science, history, math, and English.

One Teacher's Personal Reflection on the Importance of Roundtables

by Sarvenaz Zelkha

When Barack Obama became our 44th president, the nation sang in celebration of change and the world watched as he became the first black president of the United States of America. At ESCHS, the middle and high school all gathered in the auditorium to watch the inauguration live. All 550 students and the entire staff watched on a huge screen that dominated the stage.

I had an out-of-body experience when I saw the majority of our seventh-grade students, who are mostly Latino and African American, sit bored out of their minds. The middle school teachers had all taught exciting election curriculums giving our students access to news coverage, understanding the debates, and deciding which candidate they would vote for. My students had passionate debates over issues the nation was discussing such as the war in Iraq, health care, and the economy. All my students were taught the significance of having a black president given our country's history of racism. Most of them did well on their election project that proved they understood the importance of this election.

Yet on the day of the inauguration, my twelve-year-old students were bored and uncaring. When we returned to the classroom, I asked them about this and a few said, "My life is not going to change because we have a black president. Obama's life has changed, not mine." Some listed all of the successful black leaders who have been killed in this country and predicted that President Obama would be assassinated before he could make any changes. In his book *Teaching Reading to Black Adolescent Males,* Alfred Tatum writes about this invisibility that many of our students of color face, especially black male students, and how they bring this with them to the learning environment:

> During early adolescence poor black males become aware of the biting divide between how they live and how the rest of American society lives. Also during this period, seeds of despair, crime, joblessness, incarceration, and death take root. It is easy for many young black males to conclude that the world is indifferent to their existence. (6)

My students felt that drugs, violence, and gang influence would not be addressed by any president and that the government of the United States does not care about them, so why should they care about taking part in such a government?

I was silenced and shocked. What could I say? I am a Middle Eastern, Jewish woman who has always felt a sense of entitlement in the United States, even after September 11th! I was raised in a middle-class neighborhood in Queens, New York. My home was right across the street from a police station. My family always felt like the police worked for us and that we could go to them if we needed protection. Gangs and drugs did affect my middle and high school experience, but it was something on the sidelines and did not keep me from having a positive self-image as someone who this country relied on to do great things. I wanted to be someone important and make a contribution to society from the early age of twelve.

Yet my students at this same age were already discouraged and lethargic about their lives. It seemed as though no moment in history could change the impending doom of their futures—to be stuck in the projects and face the same challenges as their families.

In January, my humanities roundtables were attended by five parents, six teachers, a school administrator, two teachers from a neighboring school, two NYU student teachers, and the principal. My students were divided into groups of threes, and at least two or more adults sat in each group. After thanking all of the guests for attending the roundtables and explaining the procedures, we made a plea for help from the adults. We explained that even though the election unit went well and every student could be expected to have the project show what they'd learned and their development of their opinions, students were suffering serious detachment from the political process. "Our students know how the president got into office and have followed the elections closely. We can guarantee that they are very knowledgeable about this area of study. Yet we also know that it doesn't matter to them. The country is feeling hopeful and prideful about choosing their first African American president, but our students are in despair over their own day-to-day problems. They do not feel visible in America. Today we need you to really see our students and not just their work. We need you to connect their accomplishments in this classroom with their sense of empowerment. We need you to speak to them about the hopes we have for this nation and how they are the hands that will create that change. Apparently, the election unit did not do the job. Please help today in raising our young people to have hope for themselves."

The adults at each table were flabbergasted to hear of the issues of invisibility many of the students felt. The conversations that followed about students' achievements in the classroom and their work habits and goals for the next semester were conducted with a sense of urgency. It seemed as though every guest took special care to examine student work in the framework of how a frank discussion about students' developing identities could help them develop a more positive attitude about their future.

We accepted that the curriculum covering the elections had included important information but had not inspired the students. They simply learned information, but it did not translate into an agent of change. Instead of feeling frustrated and disappointed, we opened the issue to the community and asked for their help. In this way, the roundtables are a holistic assessment of the students' work, their skills, and their identity. At the same time, they can be an assessment of each unit of study and our responsibility to student learning; roundtables prove that learned information can be used as an agent of change in the communities in which our students live.

Some guests had serious conversations with my students and listened to their views after reviewing their accomplishments. Adults engaged students in conversations about how their developing skills were empowering. The honor roll students had some time during this assessment process to consider how being a strong reader and writer could be empowering to their lives. This may have been the first time some of the students honestly opened up and said how detached they felt from planning their own futures. When the guests evaluated the achievements each student made and celebrated their work, they did so within the framework of empowering young people to believe in their own abilities. When the guests helped students reflect on their lack of achievement in the classroom, issues of invisibility were broached, possibly for the first time in my students' lives. All work and progress were assessed, but there was a layer of honest conversation at the roundtables that began the transformative possibilities that had been a missing element in the classroom for the election unit. The roundtables assessed student work and progress and uncovered complex issues around social and emotional development that can complicate classroom learning if not addressed. As teachers we became more sincere about wanting to plan for transformative learning experiences rather than simply cover information. We were forced to be reflective about other units of study and pushed ourselves for deeper ideas. Every student came back to class the next day and we started our new units of studies. But we moved forward, enlightened about what we needed to do for students to develop their skills and to create transformative possibilities in our learning community.

3

The Middle School Roundtable

Getting Started

At ESCHS, the sixth graders hear about roundtables as a form of assessment for the first time in January. By this time they are more at ease with their status as the youngest and smallest students in the building. They have adapted with relative ease to the new middle school routine of changing classrooms with the sound of the bell and have become accustomed to the expectations of our school community.

In the classroom, on each desk, we place the individual folder that holds a student's previously graded completed exhibitions. All of the students recognize these folders and have different reactions to them. A few of the competitive students line up their folders to see who has the thickest one proving to them who did the most work. Across the room, best friends choose to compare their grades on each project, proving to them who is the better student. Most of the students just open their folder and look over their completed projects—artifacts of their learning from September to January.

"We're handing back your exhibition folder because it's time to prepare for your January roundtables, which are coming in one week." Since September, every subject teacher has made students aware that twice during the school year an event referred to as the roundtables will interrupt their normal school routine to celebrate their accomplishments. They know that a panel consisting of their classmates, a teacher or administrator, and parents will evaluate their portfolio folder. The definition of roundtables is familiar to them, but the idea that it's a celebration of their accomplishments is not so obvious. At this point, many can't envision this moment and debate what kind of celebration lacks pizza, soda, and music.

"In a few weeks something special will happen in this classroom. We will have the honor of showing everyone how smart you are and how hard you've all worked. We are so proud of your accomplishments, and we want everyone in school to know about it." Some of the kids are understandably leery and want to know what the catch is.

"In this school we don't believe that a test will always show how smart someone is. After all, it's a bunch of questions on a page that you have to answer. It can show that you're good at answering multiple-choice questions, but it doesn't give you a chance to use real information in the real world." We see a few nods. Some class time had been used to prepare for the English language arts test they will be taking in two weeks. Many students acknowledged how boring the reading selections were in comparison to their independent reading books.

"At East Side we want to celebrate how much you know. There are adults in the building who want to talk to you about the books you're reading, the stories you've written, and how much your skills have improved." This causes a stir in the room. The sixth graders want to know who will be invited to speak to them, do they have to do this, and what if they don't want to share their work with anyone.

"A lot of the adults in this building, like your other subject teachers and the administration, wonder what you enjoy reading and how your writing skills are coming along. We've told them great things about this class, and they want to see it for themselves."

Even though there is apprehension, excitement, and curiosity in the classroom, the students are thinking about themselves as learners and wondering what they have to offer in a conversation with an adult about their work. We know not everyone is up for this experience because, for a few of them, every day in my classroom has been a challenge.

"We also know this might be scary for some of you who often found it hard to finish your work and get through this class. But the roundtables are a time when you can talk to an adult about what makes this classroom hard, so that we can understand your point of view. It's a chance to be understood and supported, instead of being told that you're not good enough. Everyone has things they can improve about themselves, and this is a time to reflect on yourself as a learner." There are more questions, but we have answers to most of them. This will not be a test. It's something new. We promise them that no one is out to get them.

"Remember, this will be a celebration of you as learners before the semester finishes. I'm very excited for you. So let's begin with our preparations."

This is a new way for students to view themselves and the adults in the school building. Roundtables should be something that students desire to do well on because of the positive approach we take to them. The sixth graders review their work and wonder what they can show off about themselves as learners.

Why Does the Middle School Value Roundtable Assessments?

Most educators have accepted the idea of creating interesting and engaging lessons for our students. We go out of our way to incorporate different learning styles and individual educational plans into learning spaces to make our teaching inspirational and fun. The ultimate goal is to ensure that the information will "stick" and our students will progress.

Yet, so often when we assess our students, all of our ingenuity ceases and we give the old-fashioned test in the hope that it will take the entire class time for students to complete. To exacerbate this problem, students must take high-stakes city and state exams. Their one-shot performance on these tests can determine whether they are legally allowed to move on to the next grade. We rely on the scores of these tests to tell us how well our students are learning and if they can apply certain skills.

Even worse, we rely on these tests to inform our future curriculum. Yet a diverse student population combined with our diverse teaching strategies needs to be complemented with engaging and more authentic assessment to fully reveal what our students have learned. As part of a survey conducted in May 2007 by the New York Performance Standards Consortium to gauge parent satisfaction with their child's school, the data were compared to the parent responses in a 2006 Gallup poll regarding public opinion of the nation's public schools. Results indicated that only 8.1 percent of consortium parents and only 17.0 percent of Gallup respondents believed that the percentage of students passing state tests was a better measure than improvements shown by students during the school year when measuring the performance of their child's school (www.performance assessment.org/consequences/cparents.html).

At East Side Community High School, we use roundtables as our final form of assessment for each semester. A student's performance on roundtable day is equivalent to the traditional mid-term or final exam. The assessment takes up the entire class time. Instead of a somber test day, the roundtable day is an alternative assessment for students to show what they have learned at the end of each semester. This alternative assessment takes place in January and June. This is a time to assess student work and their progress. It is also a more accurate way to give a fair grade because a committee can decipher how much a student has learned and how well they can apply their skills.

The goal of the humanities roundtable in middle school is to give students a chance to showcase their best work, as well as work they have struggled with. The work presented at the roundtables should be representative of their overall performance. It is also a time for students to discuss their interests and growth as readers, writers, and historians. Having these conversations with peers and adults who are looking at their work allows students to be self-reflective about their choices, their achievements, and their work habits. The self-reflective quality of conversation at the roundtables can help students make adjustments in the future choices they make for themselves in school.

The roundtables are an assessment that the students believe in and really desire to do well in because their actual work is on display. They receive genuine attention, interest, and respect for all their hard work. As previously mentioned, the roundtables are attended by the students' peers, family members, and teachers from other grades.

In addition to being an alternative assessment of skills and academic progress, the roundtable process is an empowering moment when students reveal their thoughts and opinions about themselves in an academic setting. It's in middle school that issues around identity and feelings of empowerment begin to develop. We expect our students to start visualizing their futures, seeing themselves in various professions, and identifying the academic path they need to adhere to in order to reach their short- and long-term goals. But students whose families and selves have been disenfranchised in their communities have a constant struggle to develop a positive self-identity, to see themselves as being academic, and to believe that they can be empowered citizens. To strengthen variables in the classroom that help students develop the skills to make empowering decisions, believe in their abilities in an academic context, and learn how to be self-reflective about past decisions, it's important for teachers to acknowledge "that developing skills, increasing tests scores, and nurturing students' identity are fundamentally compatible" (Tatum 20).

Students show their portfolio work and have to defend the knowledge they have gained from each project. Portfolios include final projects as well as a cover letter. In the cover letter, students reflect on their work habits, the knowledge they've gained from each project, and how their skills have improved. The roundtable guests share a common goal of understanding what students have learned and determining whether they can apply this knowledge. Students are held accountable for their learning because they must be able to show their projects and speak fluently about the information learned and their process in getting the work done.

The subject teacher is also held accountable, because the curriculum, student work, and process become transparent to everyone attending the roundtables. It is most important that parents understand the curriculum goals because they are then more likely to be able to support their child's progress and have the confidence to discuss their child's academic goals with the teacher. Parents who attend the roundtables feel they are part of the learning community and have ownership over their child's progress. Once they understand the curriculum and see how their child is doing in comparison to his or her peers, they are more motivated to email the teacher with concerns, share how the child is having difficulties getting work done at home, motivate their child to stay in after school, and attend report card meetings. This dialogue between teachers, parents, and other caretakers is invaluable because it allows us to interact more authentically with the community we serve by building a relationship that celebrates each student and strives to understand their particular needs.

Overview of the Middle School Roundtables

The official school schedule for the entire grade has been rearranged to accommodate a two-hour roundtable event. At each roundtable, small groups of typically four students are expected to present their work to one another, with at least one staff member from the school and family members joining this group. Everyone sits in a circle, creating an intimate group that is focused on examining student work. Each student presents his or her work in a formal and prescribed manner for twenty-five to thirty minutes. When one student is presenting, the other three students take on the role of guests. They are expected to behave in a serious manner by reviewing the work of the presenter, asking questions, and filling out the presentation rubric to give feedback to the student presenter.

The roundtable agenda clearly outlines the goal of each step in the assessment process and how much time should be given for each task (Handout 3.1). An adult at each table, preferably a school staff member takes on the responsibility of group leader to make sure each student gets an equal amount of presenting time and that the agenda is carried through as outlined in the handout.

In most cases, the subject teacher will thank everyone for attending the roundtables and give a brief overview of what students have studied and learned during the semester. The subject teacher then takes a few minutes to review the agenda and rubric used to evaluate each student. Everyone introduces him- or herself in their small group, and the presentations begin by having the first student read his or her cover letter. Cover letters are an in-depth reflection of a student's learning. Following the reading, the student shows all of his or her notebooks and projects. Each project must include a final product and all the handouts, drafts, and revisions it took to accomplish the project. The roundtable guests look over the work and write on the reflection sheet what they notice about the presenting student's abilities, as well as any questions they may have.

The presentation rubric (Handout 3.2) is easy for students and adults to use. There is ample room within the box for guests to take notes on what they notice as they review the work. Simple sentence starters help guests organize their ideas into useful comments that can ignite an interesting roundtable discussion.

The majority of the rubric is designed to get people talking about the learning that has occurred and to keep the conversation grounded in the student work being examined. The bottom part of the rubric is a more direct grading process that assesses the oral and presentation skills of each student. The "thinking box" and scaled rubric are used not only to grade students, but also to help guests enter the conversation with some insight into the student's work process.

After quietly reviewing the work, everyone sitting in the group asks the presenting student questions. The student is responsible for defending the work and showing the ability to apply the skills she or he has learned. The student can use the work as evidence to show learning growth throughout the semester. For instance, Ricardo might showcase several different pieces of writing in a variety of genres written throughout the semester as evidence of how his skills and work habits have improved. Afterward, he answers questions about the relevance of each project to his progress, his work habits, and his approach to his work, as well as the information he had to learn. It is important for the guests to ask a variety of questions that challenge the presenter. Guests are handed a list of relevant questions to ensure that they are able to assess specific skills and information taught throughout the semester. To help keep them engaged, students who are not presenting are assessed on their participation in their peers' presentations.

The guest questions include those that we know students who are prepared can answer by referring to their work (Handout 3.3). Guests may use these questions as a starting point to have conversations about the work, but they are welcome to ask more authentic questions as they examine the portfolio.

During the last fifteen minutes of the roundtable, the student makes a five-minute presentation about a specific topic learned in the classroom or a set of skills he or she has improved on. After this presentation, we hold a ten-minute question-and-answer period between the student and the guests at his or her table. After this intense questioning time, all guests fill out the presentation rubric (Handout 3.2) that assesses how well the student did during this process.

What's in the Portfolio?

The portfolio is an organized collection of student work that each guest reviews to assess how well the student is learning. In the sixth-grade humanities classroom, we follow a workshop model for reading and writing. Therefore, the students will first place their reading logs and "Books I've Read" lists in their independent reading folders. They also will include the reader's notebook that contains their class notes on mini-lessons and evidence of their attempts to try out the mini-lessons during the active engagement part of the lesson. The reader's notebook also includes sticky notes and stop-and-jot notes they wrote while reading different books. These are key pieces for the roundtables because they show the students' progress toward becoming more powerful, independent readers.

To show their work in writer's workshop, they display their writer's notebook, which has many websites and lists written down as evidence of how they generate writing ideas. The notebook also contains attempts at different genres of writing, sketches, and creative ways in which students are playing with self-expression through writing. The writer's notebook is important when students try to discuss their writing life in and out of the classroom.

Also, the portfolio includes writing projects. The process of each writing project needs to be transparent. Therefore, each piece of published work needs to have:

- A website or list or outline to show how the student started the process
- Drafts that include revisions to show how the piece came along
- The final published version
- Teacher feedback and peer partner feedback to show how the student worked in a community of writers
- The teacher's rubric, which includes the project grade. This makes the teacher's expectations for the project clear to everyone at the roundtables.

It's important that the roundtable guests see the process through which the work was done. Only then can they fully understand what skills the student has mastered and which may still need to be worked on. The final outcome of the project is not the most important part, because it does not show process. The roundtables celebrate the quality of each piece, but they also applaud each step of the process. Roundtable assessment can also call into question the students who have incomplete projects and help pinpoint at what point they were unable to move forward with their learning. This process enforces the value of positive work habits. It also sheds light on when a lack of strong work habits perpetually cause a student to fall behind or become unable to move forward with a project.

Last, students incorporate notes, tests, and projects that may have been completed during the history portion of the humanities class. Since we expect students to learn and retain some specific historical information, it is appropriate for the guests to look over the tests and ask students some of the test questions again. The roundtables are not meant to be a moment of interrogation by any guest, but it is appropriate to hold students accountable for remembering certain dates, names, and terms that were taught in class. This discussion is most useful when the guests start historical discussions and invite students to add their point of view. This allows students to prove their knowledge and apply it to support their opinion. In the best of these discussions, we hope to hear our students speak of transformative learning and connections they make to their own identities after they have studied a certain period in history. If students don't connect to their learning, the roundtables provide the opportunity for teachers, students, administrators, and community members to reflect on the curriculum in a proactive manner. The roundtables bring the African proverb that "it takes a village to raise a child" to the teaching practice of our inner-city schools.

The portfolio can be as simple as work placed neatly in a folder or it can be as sophisticated as work placed in a binder with a plastic covering. Either way, students should be able to easily separate the reading, writing, and history sections to show all the guests different pieces at the same time. It is also important for students to bring all the notebooks and folders that hold their notes because these are evidence of their work habits in class.

Cover Letters

The purpose of the cover letter is to encourage students to be reflective learners. By writing the cover letter, students reflect on their learning and use their actual work to prove what they have learned. We guide students to use quantitative data, such as their attendance percentage, test scores, and grades on projects, to show their accomplishments in class. They also use qualitative data, such as their revision decisions on different assignments, their ability to think about literature, and their work habits, to demonstrate how their skills are improving.

In writing the cover letter, students have to be able to assess their own data to show how they are learning. Each paragraph of the letter contains some quantitative and some qualitative data that allow students to explain how they did in a class. The cover letter outline is a tool students can use to help reflect on their learning (see Handout 3.4).

Students decide how many of the questions they need to address to reflect on their learning. Also, more independent writers may choose to reorganize the outline to help craft their point more clearly.

The writing style for the cover letter needs to be formal and reflective about what students have learned about writing throughout the semester. Every year we teach students about strong leads for their narrative writing and to use evidence to back up their point of view in essays. The cover letter needs to show how students can handle both of these skills. We also teach them how to edit and proofread before publishing a piece of writing. Therefore, the semester of teaching has created a clear expectation that the cover letter be not only reflective but also well written. The length of the cover letter is not as important as how well students are able to analyze their strengths and weaknesses as learners. We can see from the excerpt of Johnny Collado's cover letter (Example 3.1) how he is using his narrative writing skills to tell the story of how he has matured as a student.

Johnny explains that he is becoming a more independent learner, that he is appreciating his ability to think more deeply about a unit of study, and that he understands the value of working on his reading skills. It is impressive when a student can assess his own learning needs and articulate what can make him more successful in the future. Eloiza Miranda's cover letter (Example 3.2) helps explain to outside guests her inner motivation to do well in school. Eloiza makes clear to the guests and herself that she can depend on her teacher to encourage her to be a better student. She connects with the idea that as a better student, she will one day have options for her life that are more optimistic than the living conditions she presently faces would suggest.

Cover letters can also be a place where students think about patterns in their work habits that might be holding them back. Victor Sanchez's cover letter (Example 3.3) exhibits a moment of reflection on how a pattern in his work habits keeps him from being a more successful student. He comes to realize that he loses his motivation in the middle of the school year and then has to spend the last two months of school making up work instead of getting ahead. The hope is that as Victor writes his cover letter and discusses his work habits with guests at the roundtables, he will be more aware when he faces this situation again. By having to write a cover letter in both January and June, students have two opportunities to look over their progress, skills, and work habits to better understand how to make more successful decisions in the classroom. This element of the roundtables—the opportunity to become a reflective learner—is one of the most valuable aspects of this assessment, and the cover letter is a space for students to do that thinking.

Prove You Learned It!

As students finish their cover letter and put their collection of work into a neat portfolio, they develop a good idea of the ways in which they have most improved during the semester. The time they have to reflect on their work and write their cover letters usually gives them a genuine clarity about themselves as learners. As their teachers, we want to notice this moment, either through a conference or by reading drafts of their cover letters. Students *need* to know by this point what skills they have improved on or mastered. An important question we ask our students is, "What were you not good at in the beginning of the semester that you are much better at now?" We give students five to ten minutes to review their portfolios and write their answers on an index card. They may work with a peer partner to help figure this out. We confer with each of them individually to make sure they have focused on a valuable skill that has been taught in class, and that they have plenty of evidence from throughout the semester to prove their point. During the conference we allow students to lead us through their learning process. We look to see if they can identify their weaknesses and track them throughout different assignments. We help them sort through their notes, revisions, and logs to find two to three significant pieces of evidence from throughout the semester that demonstrate how they slowly improved on the skill or set of skills. Once students have indicated an improved skill and have found their evidence, they need to create a poster presentation that provides the guests with a visual of their accomplishments. Students also need to prepare what they will say during their presentation and how they will use the poster.

Life Lessons

The process of making these posters and preparing their presentations can teach our students many important life lessons. The most important lesson they learn is that when a person tries to improve him- or herself, it takes a lot of work and it usually happens slowly. Our young people sometimes underestimate how much effort it takes to change something in themselves or in their lives. They get to see how their hard work throughout the semester paid off and has made them stronger students. They also get to think about what helped them the most to improve. Once students know what in the classroom is working for them, they are more likely to find relevance in the lessons and in their general classroom experiences.

Another life lesson is the ability to notice their own weaknesses as learners and be willing to work on them. Many of our students are afraid to confront the truth about their skills because they know they are not on grade level. Students connect school experiences with feelings of shame. Therefore, it's empowering for them to see that though they may not have been good at something in the beginning of the semester, through hard work they have come far in improving that skill.

As teachers who serve in communities made up of low-income and disenfranchised students, we consider it a political imperative to empower our students power by showing them how to assess themselves honestly and what they can do to change their position in the world. Our young people often feel disrespected, with no voice in their homes and community. They often feel angry about how they are treated, as well as powerless to make any change. The roundtable presentation can show them how they have full control over their learning. Perhaps for the first time, they realize that their education and willingness to work on their skills make them more powerful, and that they as young people can be catalysts for change in their community.

As the students begin to print out their cover letters and give them a final proofread in the computer lab, we pull them aside individually for a five-minute conference. We ask them to tell us what skill or set of skills they have improved on the most. We briefly go over where they might find their evidence. It's important to make time for these conferences and let the students know that in two days they need to check back in to make sure they are on the right path. We keep track of what has been discussed on index cards and make sure to write down the skill the student is focusing on. When we check back with the student in a day or two, we write down the specific pieces of evidence they have collected to prove what they have improved on. After a few days, we collect all their evidence and make copies of it for them. This way, their portfolio remains organized and they are free to design their poster in a more creative manner. Handout 3.5, Prove You Learned It!, is a document students can use as a scaffold to organize their poster. The handout includes a suggested list of questions they can use to prove what they've learned and a step-by-step guideline for how to organize their work. We also show them a model poster created by a former student and have them explain what they like about it. Having them judge a poster serves as a model of how the guests will review their work at the roundtables.

During this preparation time, we introduce students to the art of a good presentation. We put out art supplies and give them suggestions for how to decorate their posters in a way that highlights their work instead of disguising it. We discuss the role of a clean visual and clear communication. We also discuss the value of typing out the text on the posters instead of handwriting it and how they should never glue anything down until they have all their pieces pulled together.

Students have three full class days to design their posters. Anyone who finishes early gets pulled aside for a quick tutorial on how to speak clearly, where to stand, and how to use the poster in an effective manner.

How Do We Get Roundtable Guests?

Roundtable guests make students feel important and are the most important ingredient in a successful experience. We've discovered that the best configuration for roundtable groups is the following: three students, an administrator or teacher, and a parent. The school needs to rearrange class schedules or the schedule of the entire grade to accommodate the roundtable event. In the best scenario, the entire grade is doing roundtables within a two-week period so a special schedule can be drawn up for this event. Either way, the administration needs to be cooperative in allowing the teachers to create this schedule, and teachers need to work as a team to support one another to ensure that each roundtable event feels like a celebration of student work.

This special schedule also should make it possible for teachers from other grades to sit in as guests to evaluate student work. This intervisitation of teachers as guests to one another's roundtables is valuable because our students' progress and challenges are being noticed by a community of educators. Also, the presence of administrators, the school counselor, the parent coordinator, and school support staff is essential. The willingness of all these people to get to know students as reflective learners highlights the value of student work and students accountable to the school community, not just the subject teacher.

Roundtables can be a moving experience for family members. They get to hear their children speak about their work using academic language and take pride in their projects. It is often the first time a family member gets to experience how students can talk about their learning processes and understand what motivates them as life learners. We remember the first time a student's father came to her roundtables dressed in a suit. He was proud to be invited to his daughter's roundtable and to be introduced by her to the other guests.

Many parents look over the student's reading log and say in astonishment, "I never knew you read so much!" or they look at their child's writer's notebook and say, "You write so beautifully. I never knew you could write like this." This pride and astonishment is the most beautiful part of celebrating our students. The roundtables bring a child's education to the forefront of family conversation and get family members to take time to focus on the student's accomplishments.

For students who are not progressing as well as expected, the presence of a family member can be stressful. Many times family members can see what other students are accomplishing in the class and compare that with their child's work. It usually alerts them to the fact that the student needs extra help. We've heard family members asking the student, "Why aren't you doing your work?" or "How come you are not finishing what you start?" The time that family members take to look at the student's work with the other guests can start useful conversations about different strategies the student can apply to be a more successful learner. Suddenly, a student goes from shamefully not doing well to having a group of students and adults who are taking an interest in his or her issues in the classroom. Family members who attend roundtables are more likely to know how to talk to the young person about his or her academic work, to be more tuned in to what is being taught, and to understand the teacher's expectations. Family members also can try at home a variety of strategies that have been discussed at the roundtables to support the classroom learning.

It is not necessary to have all of our students' family members attend all roundtables. What we have found works best is to send home a form, such as the one in Example 3.4, and have the parent choose which subject roundtables they wish to attend. Once they have returned the form, the subject area teacher should make calls home to confirm that the family member will be in attendance and knows how to get to the classroom.

One approach we have tried is calling the homes of at least fifteen parents who we know are active in their children's lives. We personally invite them to participate and explain why we want them to attend the roundtable. Sometimes we want them to attend because of their child's magnificent achievements, and we want their child to be recognized for his or her efforts. Other times, we want parents who have been working tirelessly to help their child improve in school with little result, because we think they can benefit from the perspectives of the other guests who are examining the child's work.

If a child is having particular family issues or the presence of a family member in school will aggravate issues at home, we make sure there is an extra teacher or administrator who can sit in on the committee instead of bringing in family. Also, we encourage students to invite community members they are close to, such as a neighbor who helps raise them, church leaders, or counselors they might be working with outside of the school community.

Gathering Support for Roundtables

In attempting to implement roundtables for the first time, teachers may face many challenges. Administration may not be immediately on board with the idea of changing the school schedule for an alternative assessment process they are not familiar with. Also, other staff members may not appreciate having their schedule changed to sit at a roundtable, no matter how great the experience may be. It is important to have supportive administration because no single teacher can make a schoolwide roundtable experience possible. Roundtables are a team effort that includes an administration that accepts roundtables as an alternative assessment that has value in the learning community. This effort also takes teachers who understand how roundtables can celebrate their students even as they provide a more authentic assessment of students' skills.

If you need to ease into roundtables to show your learning community the value of this process, a less disruptive form of roundtables can be implemented temporarily until more support is forthcoming. The following ideas and structure can be followed even if a teacher has forty-five-minute periods with thirty students in each class. Each roundtable group can consist of four students who present their work for ten minutes each. Alternatively, each student can present his or her work for longer periods of time by completing the roundtables over the course of two days.

One teacher can pilot a roundtable to show the rest of the staff how it can work. Administration and teachers might stop by for a few minutes to see how it goes in the classroom. Also, the teacher might have a colleague videotape the pilot roundtable and review it with the rest of the staff at a scheduled meeting to inform the community about alternative assessment possibilities.

In doing a pilot roundtable, the students show their work for a shorter amount of time, with the goal of showing how they have grown as learners. For this pilot roundtable, students can write a shorter cover letter and share it with the group. Also, it isn't necessary to show the guests every folder and notebook. Students might show two to three pieces of major work (for example, a project, a major test, an important essay etc.) from over the course of the semester to show growth as learners. Students are responsible for being self-reflective in the cover letter, speaking about their growth as learners and using their work as evidence. In this way, students can essentially run their own roundtable experience with no outside guests. The teacher might designate one student as group leader. Group leaders are responsible for getting the other students to follow the roundtable procedures, but also will present their work when their turn comes up. If group leaders are successful with this double task, the teacher may give these students extra credit. After each presentation, which may last ten to fifteen minutes, the other students fill out the presentation rubric.

Ultimately, however, roundtables are most powerful as opportunities for a community to reflect on each student's learning, and this is enhanced through the presence of outside guests. For the purpose of creating an authentic pilot roundtable, the teacher can give extra credit to students who motivate their parents or family members to come in for the event. The teacher can invite colleagues from other grades and/or schools. The teacher can invite older students from other grades who they may have taught in the past. If the school has strong ties with other community organizations that serve the school, the teacher can invite their staff members to come celebrate the students' learning. Also, retired teachers who have served in the school may appreciate an invitation to a roundtable and can serve as reliable group leaders.

Even if a school has made the decision to place greater value on more traditional models of assessment, it is invaluable for student learning to assess students in an authentic, alternative manner alongside traditional methods to give students a chance to reflect on themselves as learners. A pilot roundtable is a good way to give students a chance to be more self-reflective while showing the staff how this can look in each classroom.

Reflective Educators

The process of roundtables is powerful for teachers because we get to see how our curriculum is shaping the lives of young adults. It is a satisfying moment to see our students speak about their favorite books and authors that we helped them discover. It's enjoyable to see a student being celebrated by others for creative writing he or she produced because of our instruction. After parents review their child's work, they are empowered by how much they understand about their child's skills and work habits. Roundtables also make it easier to know what is not working in our classrooms and how to make effective changes, because administrators are taking time to really see how students are responding to the curriculum rather than simply looking at high-stakes test scores. Overall, roundtables bring a school community together to understand how effectively we teach our students through a more organic approach to assessment.

4

The High School Roundtable

The Goals of the High School Roundtable: Student Engagement through Relevant Assessment

Just as in the middle school, each high school English roundtable features the reading of a cover letter, an exploration of student work, and a discussion and a demonstration of the mastery of skills. Every East Side staff member serves as roundtable facilitators for three of the four sessions held each day. This is a time for reflection, celebration, and nerves as students scramble to complete their cover letters, organize their portfolios, and speak as intellectuals in front of adults.

Each component of the high school English roundtable, from cover letter and portfolio to dialogue and demonstration of skills, serves a specific purpose. But the roundtable, taken as a whole, also plays several important roles for the students and the school community. Perhaps most fundamentally, roundtables remind students that the purpose of school is not simply to perform tasks in the classroom but to become critical thinkers, able to analyze the world around them and use the skills learned in the classroom to more powerfully connect and change the larger society. It is the authentic nature of this experience that helps promote the feeling that learning is relevant throughout the year.

The roundtable process tells our students that the entire school and even members of the outside community are invested in their learning. Furthermore, students do not simply complete assignments with an eye to the teacher as the sole audience; roundtables open up their work for larger consumption. We frequently push the kids by saying, "One more revision and this piece of work will be ready for your portfolio." The portfolio contains the collection of work to be shown at roundtables.

Having an interested audience lends yet another layer of relevancy to the work of our students, one that can be drawn on throughout the year. The roundtables offer students a concrete reminder of the importance of learning to express themselves clearly, both in writing and verbally. Furthermore, the roundtable demonstrates to students that their learning is applicable not just within the classroom. Adults are interested in their learning and growth, too.

Preparing Students for Roundtables

To prepare students for roundtables requires three key components, all of which must be complete for students to present. Students write a "cover letter" addressing both the themes of the course and reflecting on their growth, organize their work for the semester that earned grades of 80 or above to be included in the English portfolio, and create a presentation.

The Cover Letter

The cover letter is the focal point of the roundtable. Each roundtable begins with the adult facilitator and other group members silently reading the cover letter. The goal of the cover letter is twofold: students must demonstrate mastery of the content and reflect on what that learning has meant to them. What the student chooses to write about and the reflection he or she offers serve as the jumping-off point for subsequent discussion. The format of the cover letter is structured so that students must touch on a variety of topics, but there is enough flexibility for student voice.

For example, the curriculum of the fall semester of senior year revolves around the study of tragedy. The cover letter assignment (Handout 4.1) devotes significant time to reflecting on the key themes of the class and is an opportunity for students to demonstrate mastery of those themes and offer their own interpretations of the texts. The assignment is broken into four main sections:

> **Section 1: Tragedy.** In this section the goal is for students to synthesize the themes of the texts studied in class. Students must offer an explanation for why people read tragedies and which best captures human nature.
>
> **Section 2: Important Texts.** Considering all the texts they read over the course of the semester, students must decide which is important for others to read and explain why using evidence.
>
> **Section 3: Independent Reading.** Students describe an independent reading book they loved and analyze why they enjoyed it.

Section 4: You as an English Student. Here students must reflect on their growth and continued struggles as students of English. They discuss the assignment that mattered the most to them personally and set goals for the future.

Throughout the preparation for roundtables, students are invited to reflect on the work that means the most to them. The cover letter assignment explicitly asks students to expound on the text and assignment that resonated most with them, and often the facilitator will request to see the assignment of which the student feels most proud. This improves student engagement because students are encouraged to highlight their strengths and consider what in their learning matters most to them.

Michele and Cherrie, both seniors, selected *Oedipus* and *Othello*, respectively, as an important text for others to read. Next are excerpts from their cover letters defending their opinions. Michele defended *Oedipus* as an important text, arguing,

> We can learn from Oedipus's flaws. He was a very stubborn man who believed he was better than everyone. He always believed he was right and talked down to people. I believe that the choices he made throughout his life are what made him sleep with his mother and murder his father. It was not fate that led to his demise. People can learn that choices you make in your life will either give you consequence or rewards. But besides affecting you, they will affect those around you.

Cherrie, however, argued for the importance of *Othello*, writing,

> Because of Othello's race and outsider status, it was easy for others to manipulate him to feel jealous of his own wife and kill her in the end. This play is important because it teaches people about the danger of jealousy and how this emotion can turn people into monsters who want to destroy others.

A shy twelfth grader, Michele wrote proudly in her cover letter:

> The most important assignment for me was the personal statement that we send to colleges. It is very important to me because I wrote about a very personal moment in my life that I never wished to discuss, but I managed to have the courage to write about it using the different writing strategies that I have learned in this class.

Corey, also in twelfth grade, chose to write about the exhibition in which he was asked to create a modern adaptation of *Antigone*. Corey explained in his cover letter why this assignment mattered to him. "I took it as an opportunity to show what I can come up with as a writer. It allowed me to dig deep into my thoughts and come up with a good idea that was creative but still captured the idea of *Antigone*." Students are asked not only to demonstrate learning and growth but also to reflect on what they value about their own abilities and development.

Because of the roundtable at the end of each semester, students know they are responsible for retaining their understanding of the themes, texts, vocabulary, and skills they learn, not just for completing the assessment at the end of a unit. Learning is about long-term retention at least until the end of the term. The roundtable requires students to draw on their learning from the whole term in the completion of the cover letter and in the dialogue with the facilitator.

Students proofread their cover letters carefully because these are documents intended for public consumption.

The Portfolio

The portfolio is the collection of student work that each student begins to gather in ninth grade. Completing the "portfolio matrix" (Handout 4.2) is a graduation requirement, with each year of English having its own set of requirements. Students present their twelfth-grade work in the portfolio at the roundtable.

Only papers that earn an 80 or above are eligible for inclusion. This pushes students to revise their work, perhaps even multiple times, to produce a portfolio that reflects their very best work. By the roundtable at the end of first semester, most seniors should be close to completing their portfolio. For the twelfth grade, students must meet the following requirements:

- one narrative piece such as the college essay
- two literary essays
- one creative writing piece
- one public speaking document
- twenty-five books completed for independent reading
- one roundtable graded at "practitioner" or above

Since each year requires students to complete at least one roundtable, the portfolio has magnified the significance of the roundtable and reinforced the perception among students that the roundtable is a high-stakes event that must be prepared for with care. Students have only two opportunities a year to earn the roundtable stamp. Completing at least one roundtable at a satisfactory level each year is now a graduation requirement.

Students prepare their portfolios all semester, and only work included in the portfolio is shown to facilitators at roundtables. Students go through all of their returned assessments, including their literary essays, college essay, and creative pieces, to determine which meet the requirements of the portfolio. Those that earned an 80 or above are placed in protective sleeves, put in the portfolio binder, and marked as complete by the teacher on the portfolio cover sheet. Organizing their work in this manner reminds students of what they have learned and how they have grown over the semester and over their years at East Side.

Presentation of Skills

In addition to the innovations around the portfolio, English teachers have created new opportunities to challenge students in the presentation component of the roundtable. The goal of this portion of the day always has been for students to demonstrate their mastery of a skill or concept. However, these discussions often felt flat. A sophomore might have made copies of the memoir he wrote during the semester and had the adults read selections while he explained the writing strategies he used in his piece. While this demonstrated that the student was able to identify key strategies and related examples in his own writing, these moments felt stiff and overly prepared. Seniors had been asked to simply select a piece of work of which they felt proud and explain why it was an exemplary piece of writing. These presentations did not open the door to challenging discussions and did not demonstrate the mastery of skills to a satisfactory degree.

Instead, the department has committed to asking students to perform an on-demand task, a more authentic reflection of learning. As Wiggins explains, "authentic assessment is true assessment of performance because we thereby learn whether students can intelligently use what they have learned in situations that increasingly approximate adult situations" (21). For months in departmental meetings we struggled to create these meaningful situations that would require students to use what they have learned, on demand and in only a few minutes. Clearly, asking the student to write an essay to demonstrate writing skills was not a productive use of time.

Teachers at each grade level strived to create more meaningful forums in which students could think critically and apply the skills they have sharpened throughout the semester. Now, having completed a study of *Macbeth* in the spring of ninth grade, students turn to the text for their presentations. To prepare for their roundtable, students select key soliloquies from the play that they then memorize. During the presentation component of the roundtable, the students perform the piece from memory and analyze its significance.

In the fall of tenth grade, students demonstrate their use of reading strategies by spending a few minutes with a challenging text that they have never seen before. The teacher hands the entire table copies of this new text as the student talks through her plan for deciphering its significance. She first reads it aloud, then to herself, underlining key words as she goes. Uncertain of the meaning of a few words, she puzzles out their definitions using context clues. In the end, she has created an analysis of the characters and their motivations and inferred several key themes of this piece. She has enacted the process that skilled readers do to decipher meaning of an unfamiliar and challenging text. Furthermore, she is able to name and rely on a series of strategies that she had been explicitly taught.

The decision to have a debate in the twelfth grade on which tragic hero is the most tragic was born out of a desire to have students think critically on their feet. Students prepare their arguments, but they do not know in advance against whom they will be debating. Students must listen carefully to their opponents, take notes, and formulate rebuttals using reasoning skills and their understanding of the texts. Having encountered six potential candidates, students demonstrate a wide range of opinions, both about who is the most tragic and what being a tragic hero even entails.

To prepare for this debate, students must consider Aristotle's definition of a tragic hero, decide which characteristics and outcomes appear most tragic to them, and build a cohesive argument with evidence from the text to support their ideas. Students are instructed to prepare a three-minute opening statement in which they lay out their main arguments. They bring in written notes for this debate, though they do not write a formal speech.

We explain to students the requirements and goals of the debate (see Handout 4.3 in the appendix for the complete assignment):

Some issues to consider:

- Aristotle's definition of a tragic hero.
- Is dying more tragic than surviving?
- Is suicide more tragic than murder?
- The smaller the flaw, the greater the tragedy?
- The greater the epiphany, the greater the tragedy?

continued

You must be able to define and explain how each applies to your character:

- Aristotle's view of a tragic hero
- Flaw (Hamartia)
- Epiphany

Goals of this debate:

- Defend your ideas with evidence.
- Understand and provide a counterargument to an alternative perspective.
- Demonstrate your understanding of two of the texts we read this semester.
- Make connections between books.
- Take effective notes to enhance your argument.

To get a sense of one student's preparation for the debate, see Example 4.1 in the appendix for twelfth grader Elizabeth's preparatory notes. Some students argue passionately for Antigone's nobility. Her heroic burial of her scorned brother elevates her status, as does her dignity. But another student will hew more closely to Aristotle's definition, insisting that the hubris of Oedipus, coupled with the same hubris of his father who sought his death as an infant, creates a situation that is unbearably tragic, and with offspring to suffer the consequences. It is amazing to hear the clusters of students locked in heated argument throughout the room, needing little adult prodding to challenge one another's ideas using textual evidence.

Seniors are given three class periods to work on their cover letters—two periods to prepare for the debate and one during the last class before the roundtables when each student reviews the work in her or his portfolio. The student places three copies of the cover letter and the notes for the debate in the front pocket of the portfolio binder for easy access.

What the Roundtable Looks Like

The classroom is littered with clusters of four desks for each group (up to seven) in each class. At each table of desks, three twelfth-grade students sit with an adult facilitator. The adult may be their eighth-grade English teacher, the guidance counselor, a curious teacher from another school, or a college friend who spends her days toiling as a corporate lawyer. Each group spends ninety minutes challenging, reflecting, and celebrating the work and ideas of the students. This process repeats four times so that each of the four senior English classes has a roundtable.

At the start of each session, we quickly run guests and students through the procedure of the day (see Handout 4.4 for a reproducible "Instructions for Students and Visitors" sheet in the appendix).

1. **Reading Student Cover Letter and Reviewing Student Portfolio (10 minutes):** Participants read cover letter to themselves. After reading the cover letter, participants closely examine the work inside the student's portfolio.

   Record on the evaluation sheet comments and questions for the student generated by what you read in the cover letter and observe in the portfolio. These questions will help stimulate dialogue in the next section of the roundtable.

2. **Dialogue (12 minutes):** All participants (adults and peers) ask the presenting student questions raised by the cover letter and the work in the portfolio. Questions can relate to the content of the course, specific assignments, issues raised in the cover letter, and the student's learning process and growth. Questions may be addressed to all students at the roundtable to facilitate a group discussion. Please consult the essential questions and discussion ideas sheet for suggestions. Please avoid questions on what makes a tragic hero, as that will be the content of the debate.

3. **Repeat steps 1 and 2 for the second and third students.**

4. **Debate (15 minutes):** All students will engage in a debate on the question, "Who is the most tragic hero?" Student 1 will present a three-minute speech on why her hero is the most tragic. Students 2 and 3 will then have two minutes to ask challenging questions. Student 2 will then have three minutes to give his speech, and Students 1 and 3 will have two minutes for questions. Repeat for Student 3. Each student should then spend one minute offering a concluding statement.

5. **Assessment and Sharing of Feedback (5 minutes):** Please use the evaluation sheet to evaluate the cover letter and presentation of each student. Participants are encouraged to share feedback with students verbally and/or allow students to read over completed evaluation sheets.

We make sure that guests understand how much time to spend looking at student work and discussing it with the student. We point them to the rubrics (Handout 4.5) that the facilitator distributes to students and collects at the end of the roundtable. The rubric is a space to record observations, provide feedback, and offer direct assessment. We explain that the facilitator and students alike will complete a rubric for each presenter. At the end of the roundtable, students have a few minutes to look over the rubric with the comments of the adult facilitator and their peers.

"We are so proud of the accomplishments of this class. They have tackled extremely challenging texts, written sophisticated literary analysis, performed scenes, and used their creativity. But do not go easy on them. They are up for the challenge and prepared to question one another, think critically, and engage in meaningful discussions on the themes of the course and their own growth and continued areas of struggle." After this brief speech, the teacher's official role has concluded. We must step back and observe the students engage in academic discussions. It is an odd feeling to be an observer in our own classrooms, but we are excited by the work our students have done and eager for the feedback from our colleagues.

The room is silent as everyone pores over the cover letter of the group's first presenter. A complete, proofread cover letter, submitted in advance, is a prerequisite for participating in the roundtable. Students and facilitators alike read through the piece and record their comments and evaluations on the first third of the rubric.

Once everyone has finished reading the cover letter, the first student presents her portfolio for perusal. The presenting student explains the context of various assignments as the group reads through the pieces.

Students may show off their literary essays on the issue of the extent to which Oedipus was a victim of his fate or of free will. They may showcase their essay exploring who or what is to blame for the death of Desdemona in *Othello* or the scenes they created that transferred the central conflict of *Antigone* into the modern world. The exploration of the work often provides a fluid transition into the dialogue with the student around the work and the class.

Questions for discussion are taped to each desk, though often the work in the portfolio and the cover letter inspire more than enough material for discussion. This component of the roundtable requires students to present an oral defense of their learning. All of the material for the semester is fair game, and the hope is that students have internalized their understanding of the material and are ready to apply it in a new situation. The questions are drawn from each unit's essential questions and the major themes we addressed in class. For example, students read both *Oedipus* and *Antigone*. The questions for Unit 2: Greek Tragedy include:

Unit 2: Greek Tragedy (*Oedipus Rex* and *Antigone*)

- Do we control our destinies?
- Is Oedipus his own worst enemy or a victim of fate?
- Why does Oedipus blind himself at the end of the play? How does Sophocles use the imagery of sight and blindness throughout the play?
- How did ideas around gender roles cause the tragedy in *Antigone?*
- Who better fits Aristotle's definition of a tragic hero: Antigone or Creon?
- What can *Grey's Anatomy* teach us about tragic heroes?

See Handout 4.6 in the appendix for the complete sheet of essential questions and discussion ideas.

For some students, the roundtable is a public reckoning. Why is there so little work in your portfolio? Why does your cover letter feel so rushed? Students are not allowed to slip through the cracks but must own up to their struggles. Often, the roundtable becomes a brainstorming session for the most struggling students on how to rectify their performance in school. The aim is not to humiliate students but rather the opposite, to offer strategies for improvement. With an adult concerned and curious to discover why a student has struggled, that student may leave the roundtable feeling motivated to do better in the next semester.

Two small moments from roundtables help illustrate the power of this assessment. Nailah, a ninth-grade English teacher, held two of Raphael's literary essays during his senior English roundtable. "Raphael, I notice that you have some great ideas and very strong introduction paragraphs. However, by the end you are barely explaining your evidence."

"Yeah," Raphael said slightly sheepishly but not at all surprised. "I tend to focus a lot on the beginning and then I rush through the end just to get the assignment done."

When reminded of his conversation with Nailah when he was working on a literary essay second semester, he replied, "I know. I'm not going to rush the ending. I already have my outline, so I think I'll be fine."

The essay Raphael produced was his strongest one of the year. He had owned the feedback from Nailah and committed to changing his work habits to produce a far superior paper.

Jen, Elizabeth's tenth-grade English teacher, said, "Elizabeth, when you were in tenth grade, I remember you completing well over twenty-five books in a semester, but in your cover letter you mention that you only finished six. This is distressing. What has happened?"

"I know. With all the stress around applying to college and keeping up with my homework, I don't have the time," Elizabeth responded.

Jen then suggested several titles that Elizabeth might enjoy. Though she did not complete as many books as she once had, Elizabeth made reading independently more of a priority in the next semester, committing to trading her iPod for a book during her commute to school. These small moments reinforce the point that every adult in the building cares about the learning of every student. They also show the way lessons and insights from roundtables push students to succeed in the future.

Every adult in the community is responsible for explaining to students how to be successful in school. This provides much needed support for the classroom teacher and once again reminds students that their learning matters far beyond the walls of one classroom. Hearing this feedback from other teachers reinforces students' understanding of what they need to improve and how they can go about making changes. So much of the power of this assessment rests in its authenticity.

After the process of reading the cover letter and looking over student work for each student is complete, the adult with each group facilitates the debate between students. The adult's role is to act as timekeeper, with the structure clearly explained on the "Directions for Students and Visitors" sheet that has been taped to each desk (see Handout 4.4). As the first student presents his argument, the other two students must take notes on his statements to best refute them. Time is built into the debate for rebuttals.

Once the debate has concluded, all participants take a few minutes to complete rubrics and share their feedback. The adult facilitator takes the lead in offering feedback both positive and critical.

The rubric offers space for feedback on each component of the roundtable and asks the facilitator to offer an overall grade. The language of the overall grade may seem odd, or overly harsh, but was adapted as a departmental decision to align with assessment terminology used throughout the school. Students are familiar with the terms *expert, practitioner, apprentice,* and *novice* from their other subjects. Obviously, other language could be substituted, such as *exceeds standard, meets standard,* or *approaches standard.*

In the twelfth grade, the roundtable impacts the students' grade as a major project, much like a literary essay, test, or substantial creative project. In the fall of twelfth grade, students are also assessed through a final exam in an effort to mimic what the students will see in college the following year. The final exam and the roundtable serve as perfect complements to each other. In preparation for the final, students reviewed the central themes of the semester and refreshed their understanding of the texts we studied. The exam asked students to identify and analyze passages and answer questions exploring themes that appeared in multiple texts. Giving students the experience of studying for an exam, refreshing their memories of the texts, and writing on demand are essential to preparing them for college. It is important that students learn to handle anxiety around tests, manage their study time, and recognize the benefits of having paid attention all along.

Nurturing Reflective Learners

By the time an East Side student arrives in twelfth-grade English, he or she has participated in upwards of forty roundtables. Unlike Sarvenaz's middle school students, who must be convinced to buy into the notion that there are adults who are interested in their work and growth, seniors are well versed in pitching their accomplishments, demonstrating what they have learned, admitting their weaknesses, and promising to do better. They are keen observers of their own growth, due in large part to this semiannual reflection in each of their subjects.

Perhaps what most distinguishes the roundtable from other forms of assessment is its emphasis on reflection on growth and learning. Both in the cover letter and during the roundtable itself, students must consider how they have grown, where they continue to struggle, and what steps they can take to ensure success in the future. The cover letter is, as Huot explains, "a reflective discourse" (76). Students discuss the assignments that meant the most to them, reflect on their areas of growth, and acknowledge weaknesses that remain to be addressed. They think about themselves as readers and writers and students. Students confess their flaws and strategize ways to improve. Next are samples from Jessica's and Cherrie's cover letters in which they explore areas of growth during their first semester of senior year. Jessica wrote,

> I have grown as a reader because of Shakespeare and Sophocles. These texts are very difficult to read, let alone understand. But that is why patience is very important. Rereading is the key. Over time the texts become easier to comprehend. I am a more fluent reader because of this challenge I was faced with.

Cherrie reflected on her growth as a writer,

> I learned how to analyze quotes deeply. It's important to know how to analyze a quote because I am using what others have said to further prove my points.

While the roundtables are obviously an oportunity for students to be assessed, as teachers we are also eager to hear the feedback of our peers. For many of our colleagues, this roundtable will be their sole chance to observe the fruits of our curriculum. Thus roundtables also provide an element of assessment and transparency for the teacher as well. Clearly, the views of the teacher guests may depend on the type of student they are grouped with, regardless of how much the discussions reveal about the choices we have made and the focus of our teaching. The successes and continued struggles of the students are certainly a reflection, at least in part, of our work as their teachers. Knowing that we are not isolated laborers locked away in a classroom, but members of a community of educators, shapes our practice throughout the year. The roundtable stands as a vivid reminder of the roles and responsibilities of the community. We are all involved, over the course of the years, in the education of these students. And we are accountable not only to our students but to our colleagues as well. Furthermore, just as the roundtable encourages students to reflect on their choices, learning, and growth during the semester, so too it encourages the teachers to similar reflection.

The roundtable, too, offers valuable preparation for college. Just as students had to write on demand for the exam, at the roundtable they must discuss ideas on demand, at times in front of a stranger. With all their practice over the years during roundtables, East Side students should have little to fear when making presentations in college classrooms or professional settings. Taken together, these two assessments beautifully round out the semester and do a thorough job of evaluating the learning of the student as a whole. Some students would prefer the exam any day, nervous about defending their ideas verbally, while others shudder at the thought of the exam, preferring the more flexible nature of the roundtable.

Perhaps most significant for our population of students, East Side graduates are imbued with the confidence that their voice matters. As Maxine Greene reminds us, "through the building of a community the ground may be laid for an articulate public empowered and encouraged to speak for itself, perhaps in many voices, within classrooms" (274). East Side's community is firmly committed to empowering students to stand up for their beliefs, ideas, and values. Our students see again and again that when they do speak, there is an entire community of adults interested in what they have to say and pushing them to work even harder and to say it even more convincingly. East Side graduates go out into the world with the knowledge that they can participate in academic discussions with ease. Their opinions deserve to be heard, and students know that they have the skills to coherently express themselves and their ideas. This agency will serve them well in college and beyond.

Finally, to give readers a sense of how this process changes as students age, and to track the growth of one student over time, we have included the cover letters Nazia wrote in the spring of each grade, eighth through eleventh, and her cover letter from January of her senior year (Example 4.2). We include them to show the continuity of the cover letter assignment across a student's career at East Side. We believe that the roundtable teaches students the power of their voice and beliefs. As the sophistication of their writing and thinking develops, we also hope to nurture a passion for the material and their own learning.

5 Authentic Formative Assessments in the High School Classroom

> Literacy is not just a desirable ideal; it is a social imperative . . . [a] precondition for students to be able to access and exercise their other civil rights, such as freedom of speech and the right to vote. . . . [S]uch literacy enables students to have a voice, take a stand, and make a difference. In other words, it gives them power. (Plaut 2)

In the fall of 2003, the eleventh-grade humanities curriculum was a clean slate to be constructed by the teachers. Because we perceived education as a political act, we created a curriculum focused on social justice through an examination of US history and American literature. At this point all students were required to take both the English Regents and the US history Regents during their eleventh-grade year. These were two very high-stakes tests that students needed to graduate from high school, and there was no denying the fact that the students felt a very high level of anxiety about these tests. The first time we asked them to do a timed essay in class, you could almost hear all of their hearts double-speed beating through their chests. We realized that our curriculum needed to be relevant to the students in a way that helped them see their education and their knowledge as a source of power. This power would allow them to excel both in their studies and on the standardized tests.

In 2005, humanities at East Side split into two separate classes, English and US history, and the students now had to take only the English Regents. Since then we have been constantly working and reworking the curriculum so that the central focus of the curriculum is for students, through their examination of literature, to examine the world they live in, including their grievances with it, and to develop their voice in writing as well as orally to speak about what matters to them, because "knowing and learning take on importance only when we are convinced it matters, it makes a difference" (Meier 173). While doing this, we held and still hold firmly to the ideals outlined in the introduction—that with a solid and rigorous English curriculum, students will be prepared to succeed on the state tests as well as to express themselves through more alternative and authentic assessments.

The Curriculum

Our curriculum has evolved from the former humanities curriculum in response to student input and feedback as well as to the changing political climate in the world. One major influencing factor in our curriculum design is the idea that "those denied entitlement to speak, be heard, and be respected inside public schools are most typically the children, adolescents, and adults of low-income, African American, and Latino communities" (Fine 25). This is the community in which we teach. Students often maintain a pretense of the attitude that "things don't matter" to keep themselves protected from the reality that they live in a society that often sends them messages making it clear that they are not valued. At the same time, they are still teenagers who want to belong, have fun, and take advantage of opportunities that come their way.

According to Michelle Fine, "school talk and knowledge [has been] radically severed from the daily realities of adolescents' lives. . . . [S]tudents [are] often encouraged to disparage the circumstances in which they [live]" (36). Our desire has been to build a curriculum in which students can use literature to access their own understanding of the world and, rather than "disparage" their realities, celebrate the positives and think about solutions for the negative. Fine continues, "The room for possibility and transformation lies with the energy of these adolescents, and with those educators creative and gutsy enough to see as their job, passion, and responsibility the political work of educating through diverse voices and nurturing communities" (52). We respect our students' realities, understanding that "American young people are presently often called upon to make the kinds of choices their elders seldom had to confront. . . . [Curriculum] must integrate certain of these concerns, as well as students' ability to cope with losses and catastrophes, into interdisciplinary curricula" (Greene 269). For us, the key is to use a wide range of literature and assessments that allow students to tap into their own imaginations, providing them with the tools to examine their own realities in a positive way. This is important, because "through the building of a community, the ground may be laid for an articulate public empowered and encouraged to speak for itself, perhaps in many voices, within classrooms" (Greene 274). The entire year at ESCHS is structured using backward design, and the end goal is for all students to feel the power of their own voice. The English Regents exam, New York's high-stakes test, occurs in the middle of the year. Rather than devote a semester or even a unit to test preparation, we know that this curriculum will provide our students with the skills they need to succeed.

When planning curriculum, we think about where we want students to be at the end of the year, and that becomes the entire focus of our curriculum planning. As we mentioned, by the end of the eleventh-grade year we want students to feel empowered to use their own voices to write and speak about the world they live in, both academically and creatively. Many students enter the classroom without a clear idea of how to make their voices heard in our society, so each unit and each assessment for the unit introduces them to ways in which other writers have chosen to examine society. This begins to give them the means to experiment with their own voices. We create each unit by first thinking about big ideas and essential questions, and then constructing assessments that will allow students to show their understanding of these big ideas and essential questions, and then, finally, creating the daily lesson plans that will help students reach the point where they are equipped with the skills and the knowledge to be successful on the summative assessment (Wiggins and McTighe 10).

Currently, the eleventh-grade English curriculum is broken down into the following five units, with essential questions that center on a particular work of literature we read as a whole class:

Unit One: Community Leadership and Identity in American Literature
Key Concepts: EMPOWERMENT, EXPLOITATION
Essential Questions:
How does *Bodega Dreams* depict the creation of identity, leadership, and dreams in East Harlem? How is the fine line between empowerment and exploitation expressed in relationship to leadership in literature? How can we use different models of short story structure to create our own stories about community leaders?
Assessment: Community leader short story exhibition

Unit Two: Revolutionary Literature
Key Concepts: INDOCTRINATION, CODE SWITCHING
Essential Questions:
How have different genres of literature been used by American authors to convey revolutionary ideas? How are the concepts of indoctrination and code switching connected to revolutionary ideas as expressed in *Kindred*?
Assessment: Multigenre revolutionary literature exhibition

Unit Three: Searching for Justice in American Literature
Key Concepts: APATHY, INEQUITY
Essential Questions:
How can different media depict the struggle for justice in the American judicial system? How are the individual rights of Americans negotiated

in literature? What is the relationship between apathy and inequity as expressed in *To Kill a Mockingbird*?
Assessment: Justice speech exhibition

Unit Four: Exploring Power in Drama
Key Concepts: DISILLUSIONMENT, COLLECTIVE VS. INDIVIDUAL
Essential Questions:
How does August Wilson use language and setting in his plays to convey the African American experience? How do disillusioned people find ways to get power, and what do they do with it when they have it? How does drama convey the ways in which one's individual as well as collective past influence the capacity to hate, as shown in *Death and the Maiden* and *The Laramie Project*?
Assessment: Theater performance exhibition and comparative paper

Unit Five: Modern Experience in American Memoir
Key Concept: DISENFRANCHISEMENT
Essential Questions:
How is the memoir *All Souls* used to express the difficulties of coming of age in a position of disenfranchisement in America?
Assessment: Testimonial exhibition

Authentic Assessments and VOICE

If the end goal is to have students feel empowered to use their own voices to write and speak about the world around them, it is imperative to create a classroom community where they feel safe doing so, so we have structured assessments throughout the year to allow them to experiment with different ways of using their voices. This has led us to create alternative assessments for each unit—the final one involving the most direct use of students' voices to speak about their own reality.

The first exhibition asks students to write a short story that focuses on a community leader:

> Having explored the relationship between leaders and their communities in *Bodega Dreams*, *The Harris Men*, and *The Lesson*, as well as how leaders choose to empower and / or exploit others and themselves, you are now going to create

your own story about a community leader. Your story should (1) be fully developed with a story arc, developed character(s), defined community setting, and conflict(s) that are resolved; (2) depict a main character who exhibits leadership qualities or holds a leadership position in the community; and (3) explicitly express whether the leader in your story EMPOWERS and/or EXPLOITS the community.

We urge students to set the story in a community with which they are familiar (their school, their home, their neighborhood, their city, etc.). In addition, they can base the leader on someone they know, but we remind them that the story should be a work of fiction. This exhibition allows the students to start thinking about the role of leaders in their community but, because it is creative, they are able to activate their imaginations and thus not feel as vulnerable as they might if they were writing true stories. When the stories are complete, students share them in small groups.

The second exhibition allows students to choose from a variety of genres to create pieces that convey revolutionary messages.

In class we have studied television shows, poems, songs, a letter, and a novel that have conveyed revolutionary messages and dealt with issues of code switching and/or indoctrination.

NOW IS YOUR TIME TO BE A REVOLUTIONARY IN YOUR OWN WAY!

Step one: Choose a TARGET ISSUE
Step two: Choose a GENRE

The genres that students can choose from are poetry, song, comic strip, or letter. When sharing with the class, we turn the room into a mini-museum, and students walk around to check out one another's work.

The third exhibition is a speech about justice.

In this exhibition you will write and present a two page typed PERSUASIVE speech that will give you your chance to define *justice* in your own terms; connect it to the texts we have studied; provide alternatives to the forms of justice that were shown in the texts, in particular *To Kill a Mockingbird*; and convince your audience of the importance of justice in our society as you have defined it.

A key in this exhibition is connecting literary analysis with students' own real-life experiences. In sharing with the class, each student must stand at a podium and deliver the speech aloud.

The fourth exhibition is a theatrical performance exhibition.

> Having studied, examined, and discussed the plays of August Wilson as pieces of literature, for this exhibition we will approach the plays through the world of performance.
>
> Every group will introduce and perform one scene for the class (memorized) with props and stage directions.

In this exhibition the students continue to work on their public speaking and performance skills. Additionally, in their written work and in the performance they must be able to make connections between the characters and themes of the scenes they are presenting and their own lives. This assessment introduces the new element of group work. As a group, students decide which roles to play and constantly push one another to stay on task. The final assessment will mirror this group structure.

The fifth exhibition is a testimonial project.

> Having seen how Michael Patrick MacDonald has used his voice to write a memoir and break the silence, over the next few days you will use your voice to write a testimonial about disenfranchisement in your community.
>
> It should make its point by telling a true story in first person. This can be from your own experience, a close friend's or relative's experience, or something you have witnessed. Think about how people can be disenfranchised by their class, race, age, gender, sexuality, ethnicity, religion, etc.

This exhibition focuses on the idea of breaking the silence and really using one's voice to speak out about the ills and injustices of society. The intention of this exhibition is not to have students disparage their communities and realities but to have them raise awareness, reject denial, and use their voices in a positive way to make sure people are aware of what is going on around them. In addition to sharing these testimonials with the class, students videotape or audiotape them and the video or podcast is produced on a webpage so students can get their words out to a larger community.

Each and every one of these exhibitions is authentic in nature while connected to the texts we study, highly relevant to the students' lives, and connected to real-world issues and/or situations. The idea is that while engaging in these assessments, students will be "enjoying a rich and critical social education . . . enabl[ing] low-income women and men to sustain, nourish, and activate their piercing and collective political commentaries, without retreating into the individualism, self-blame, and anomie that these 'older dropouts' so vividly narrated" (Fine 229). In students' end-of-year cover letters, we can see this ability to articulate such ideas. One student, Julisa, wrote: "This class has given me a new perspective on our society because truth becomes sugar coated, but in this class everything is revealed through literature. The books we have read have opened up new opinions to society along with questions." Another student, Michelle, stated, "I really enjoyed the experience of both reading breathtaking books and writing essays on them, expressing our opinions about the books and their themes. My interest as a reader has really grown this year because we have read powerful books that have opened my eyes to the world even more." And finally, James captured his experience eloquently: "Studying and discussing literature in English class has helped me in deciding where I would like to make my standpoint for the future. Shall I become the apathetic bystander who watches the world crumble? Or will I become the empathetic leader who helps rebuild the world in the likeness of a utopian society? English has helped me find a sense of myself in finding a way to combat the forces of inequality and fight for justice." All of these students' words show the kind of empowerment they have found through an examination of literature that intersected with their efforts to develop their own voices.

Balancing These Assessments with the High-Stakes English Regents Exam

One question outsiders might ask is: if the students have to take the high-stakes English Regents exam in the midst of this class, how do all of these assessments help them prepare for that? It is important to first examine what is required of students on the standardized test. The New York State Comprehensive English Regents is a four-part exam given to students over two days, for three hours each day. Session One, Part A provides the students with a five- to seven-minute listening passage from which they must gather information. They hear the passage twice and then they must answer six multiple-choice questions. They then write a response based on the prompt they are given. Session One, Part B provides students with a nonfiction (usually scientific) passage accompanied by a graph/chart or map. They must read the passage, interpret the chart, and then use information from both to answer ten multiple-choice questions and write a response based on the prompt they are given. Session Two, Part A provides students with two short literary passages. They must read, identify, and compare a common theme (controlling idea) in the two texts. After reading, they answer ten multiple-choice questions and then write an analytical literary essay. Session Two, Part B provides students with a "critical lens." This is a quote that the students must interpret and apply to their analysis of two works of literature. For this part, they must rely on their knowledge of books they have read. When considering how to ensure that students are prepared for this test while, at the same time, teaching a curriculum that includes the alternative assessments previously described for our eleventh-grade English class, it is important to look at the skills students need to succeed on the Regents compared to the skills students need to be successful on the alternative assessments. The following chart breaks down and compares the skill sets:

Skills needed to pass high-stakes English Regents exam	**Skills needed to succeed on eleventh-grade alternative and authentic assessments**
Listening	Listening
Taking notes	Taking notes
Critical reading and interpretation of nonfiction	Critical reading and interpretation of nonfiction
Critical reading and interpretation of fiction	Critical reading and interpretation of fiction
Knowledge of literary terms/elements	Knowledge of literary terms/elements
Interpretation of charts/graphs/maps	Annotating texts
Annotating texts	Organizing/outlining information
Organizing/outlining information	Analytical writing
Analytical writing	Using quotes as evidence
Using quotes as evidence	Time management
Time management	Knowledge of books read
Knowledge of books read	Knowledge of short story structure/story arc
Answering multiple-choice questions	Imagination
	Knowledge of a variety of genre structures: poetry, song, comic strip, letter
	Desire for change in society
	Use of persuasive language in a speech
	Ability to make connections between text and society
	Ability to define justice in own words
	Public speaking
	Knowledge of dramatic performance elements
	Ability to market a theater piece
	Drama interpretation
	Identifying disenfranchisement in society
	Making personal and relevant connections in writing

By creating this chart, we are able to visualize how the choices we make with the curriculum and our assessments meet the needs of students who need to be prepared to succeed on the standardized test. Being prepared means students can feel confident in approaching the test because they are equipped with the necessary skills. We do not need to "teach to the test" to instill that confidence. Rather, through the construction of a rigorous, relevant curriculum, with authentic assessments that call on students to truly show their knowledge, we provide students with the preparation they need for the test. Two elements from the Regents skill side of the chart (answering multiple-choice questions and interpreting charts/graphs/maps) are not directly addressed in the eleventh-grade English curriculum. However, they are addressed in science and math classes throughout the high school. On the other hand, there is a multitude of skills on the other side of the chart that are not tested for on the standardized test—skills such as using one's imagination, public speaking, making personal connections, identifying instances of disenfranchisement, and giving voice to a desire for change in society. Through our experiences as teachers at East Side Community High School, we recognize that these are invaluable skills that allow students to feel they are empowered members of society. It might be helpful for you to create a similar chart when devising your own assessments. First identify the skills that students will need in order to succeed on the standardized test, and then think about how you could incorporate those skills into a more authentic assessment that is connected to your curriculum.

Traditional Assessments Integrated into This Curriculum

In addition to the authentic assessments and the high-stakes, state-mandated test, we do incorporate more "traditional" formative assessments into the eleventh-grade classroom, such as short-answer quizzes, tests, and timed essays. Throughout the first semester, to help students get used to the pressure of time on state tests, all students keep an essay-writing book. In this book, they complete at least eight timed essays that reflect the prompts on the Regents exam but that are always connected to the texts we are reading in class. In addition, we provide mini-lessons on improving essay writing throughout the semester, and students keep track of these in their essay-writing notebooks as well.

During the second semester, after students have passed the state exam, "traditional" academic writing shifts to working on longer comparative papers about the literature students are reading. Using the skills they have gained on timed essays, they expand their depth of analysis and analytical skills through longer paper assignments that they will continue to work on in twelfth grade in preparation for college.

Screenplay Panel Presentation: Eleventh-Grade Alternative to Roundtables

Though eleventh-grade students have official roundtables at the end of the first semester, we have opted for an alternative assessment for the end of the year. The reason for this comes back to the idea of student voice. Students are asked to apply their voices in a variety of ways to a simulated high-pressure situation that allows them to show connections between the literature they have read, themselves, and society. This is a chance for students, in groups, to really delve deeply into the political significance of one text they have studied and prove why it is important to the world in which they live.

In the screenplay panel presentation, students must formally present to a panel of guest judges a proposal "pitch" to adapt a novel we have read as a class into a movie and persuade the panel that their proposal is worthy of being produced. Public speaking skills are developed throughout high school and especially in the eleventh-grade year. This presentation simulates a real-life experience and prepares our eleventh-grade students for the reality of job and college interviews. While the roundtables do entail public speaking, they are done in a less formal, small-group manner. After years of roundtables, students at East Side are ready for the new challenge that is more like an interrogation. This presentation is done in June (the last month of school), and the preparation time is roughly two weeks, depending on the school schedule.

The Procedure

Step One: Explaining the Project to Students and Choosing Responsibilities

Students are seated in groups of four. In their groups they are given extensive guidelines for the project (Handout 5.1) that we will break down into smaller pieces. We walk them through the expectations as outlined in the guidelines.

First, students are introduced to the idea that they will, as a group, choose a book that we have read as a class to make into a movie based on the call for proposals issued from the Power to the People film company. We explain that this is a make-believe film company, but we will approach this project as professionals, as if responding to a true call for proposals. All of the options are tied to units we studied during the year. For example, one option is a response to the key concepts and essential questions from the Modern Experience in American Memoir unit described earlier: true-life stories that depict how the failure of government services led to the disenfranchisement of certain people or a community (the memoir *All Souls* would be the book choice here).

Second, we go over the options for individual responsibility. Three written parts of the proposal need to be completed, and one student in each group should work on Part One (three-act summary, Example 5.1), one student should work on Part Two (proposal letter, Example 5.2), and two students should collaborate on Part Three (screenplay, Example 5.3). If the groups are larger than four, another option for dividing the individual work is to have two people write a letter and then the group can decide which letter is stronger to use in the presentation. This is a valuable option if you have a group in which all the individuals prefer to have their own assignment and responsibility. This also can help if one of the students in the group goes truant; if that student doesn't complete his or her work, the group will have no difficulty turning in all completed assignments. Though we want group members to feel they have ownership over the decision and their choices, we can help guide them in making these decisions by keeping these factors in mind.

Third, the students are instructed in their groups to do three things: (1) choose the proposal option; (2) divide up individual responsibilities; and (3) choose a specific scene from the selected novel to focus on for Part Three—the screenplay excerpt. When they have made these three decisions, we keep records of what each group is doing and what part each member of the group is responsible for completing. Keeping the records helps us to hold students accountable. We inform them that they should not worry about the video recording until week two, when all the other parts are complete.

Step Two: Students Drafting and Editing

This part of the procedure is highly dependent on the ability levels of students, access to computers at school and at home, and length of class periods. However, we discuss the choices we make based on the factors present in our school environment, which are as follows: (1) classes are a heterogeneous mix of levels; (2) computer resources are limited at school; and (3) about 50 percent of students have computers at home. We meet with students for fifty to fifty-five minutes every day. That being said, for this end-of-the-year presentation, students are given five full class days to complete the work for the project before preparing for the video and presentation. The five days are broken up as follows:

Day One: Work in groups brainstorming for individual work. Screenwriters meet together for a mini-lesson on screenwriting. For homework, students should complete a rough draft of their individual task.

Days Two and Three: Computer lab. Drafting and editing in class and at home for homework.

Day Four: Reconvene in groups in the classroom. Exchange and edit work, providing feedback for other group members. For homework, make final changes and edits.

Day Five: Final day in the computer lab. Students must complete final drafts of individual work and have it printed out in class or at home for the next day.

Step Three: Practice for the Presentation and Video Recording of the Scene

Practice can be broken into two or three class days, again depending on student readiness. Each group needs at least one period for the video recording and one period for practicing their presentation. Before they even begin either of these two parts, we discuss what is expected with the video recording and the presentation. This takes about half a class period and then, as they plan their recording and presentation, we devise a recording schedule for the groups. Over the next two class periods, some groups will record and some will practice their presentation.

Before discussing what happens the day of the presentation, we go over expectations for public speaking, including speaking clearly and audibly, staying focused while other people in the group are talking, speaking with confidence, being persuasive, and dressing appropriately. All of these skills have been integrated into assessments throughout the year, and this is the "final exam," so to speak, in terms of students presenting their public speaking skills.

Then we clearly outline what needs to be included in the presentation and approximate timing (each group has about twenty to thirty minutes in front of the panel):

1. All presenters must introduce themselves.
2. The letter must be read aloud from a podium.
3. The scene must be introduced from the podium so that the panel has a greater understanding of the context of the story (parts of the three-act structure can be used for this).
4. Everyone views the prerecorded scene.
5. At the end, everyone participates in question-and-answer session.

We also make it clear that each individual in the group must participate in either #2, #3, or #4. In addition, every member of the group must answer at least one question from the panel. If a student does not participate in both of these ways, he or she cannot receive a passing grade for the presentation.

After all of this has been outlined for the students, they work in their groups to prepare. They decide who will be responsible for which speaking part and then they run through it. We recommend they run through the entire process of steps at least three times without an audience. Then, during the second day (or second hour) of preparation, we have them partner up with another group, and each group runs through its pitch for the other group. All of these run-throughs happen without the question-and-answer segment.

The final step of preparation is to have each group go through a mock question-and-answer session. For this we set up four or five chairs in the front of the classroom, and each group gets a five- to seven-minute turn in the front of the class fielding questions from their peers. These questions come from a sample question sheet that is prepared for the panel guests (see Handout 5.2).

The Day of the Presentation

The Setup

We use the school library, which is an average size. The room is divided by a bookcase into one larger section and one small section. The presentations are held in the small section. A panel of "judges" sits behind a table (we'll address the role and identity of the judges later). In front of the table is a podium to one side and five chairs where the presenting group sits. The groups not presenting sit at the tables in the large section of the library until they are called to present. We use this arrangement to heighten the reality of the pressure, in the sense that groups are "waiting" with the groups they are competing against to get the money to make their movie. While the students are usually talkative and cheery, on this day the groups waiting usually sit at their tables engaged in any last-minute prep they can squeeze in.

Each class is in the library for a period of one to two hours depending on whether this is a day with a roundtable schedule or a regular schedule. Each group presents for roughly twenty minutes. If they present on a roundtable schedule, all of the groups present within the designated two-hour period. Otherwise, the presentations might be spread over two days so all groups get equal time to present.

Panelists and Their Responsibilities

We have four guest panelists for each group. Guests include teachers from the school, parents, administrators, and outside guests, ideally professionals from the film industry. Living in New York City, we have been lucky to find actors, screenwriters, and producers who are willing to sit on the panel for one day. However, we recognize this is not an option for everyone. In fact, the first year we implemented this project, we did not even consider having a true "professional" on the panel. So, to heighten the pressure in the situation and to simulate a "real" environment, we had a teacher's mother be a guest, and she was introduced as a film producer. This worked perfectly. As long as you can find someone to "act" the part of a film professional, that individual necessarily have to be in the industry.

Panelists who have not read the books are given a synopsis of each book before the presentations begin so that they are familiar with the stories and have them as a reference throughout. It is sometimes better to have at least one panelist who is not familiar with the novels because she or he tends to challenge the students by needing more in-depth explanations than someone who is familiar with the texts. In addition, panelists are coached to be serious and intimidating. We tell them we do not want them to make the students feel comfortable but rather to make them feel the pressure. And, finally, panelists are given a rating sheet to complete after each presentation (see Handout 5.3).

Watching the presentations, we are always struck by both the passion of the students and their analysis of the text. The project asks students to explore why they have connected with the novel and to consider ways in which this text will hold meaning for others. Students advocate fiercely for their adaptations. When guests ask challenging questions, the students are poised and forceful in their responses. Group members support one another during the question-and-answer session, listening carefully and thinking critically on their feet. Students are rehearsed and polished; it is easy to imagine them leading presentations as college students or in their careers. All year, students have worked to develop the power of their voices, and when they conclude this project they feel exhilarated. This is a moment for students, administrators, teachers, and outside observers to celebrate on many levels the success of this authentic assessment.

How to Adapt This to Your Curriculum

This call for proposals can be adapted to connect to any unit that is taught with a focus on the study of a novel, play, or memoir. We adapt it each year to fit the units and novels we have taught. The call for proposals is easy to adapt to fit whatever units you teach in your classroom as long as novels are at the center of the unit. The key is to develop a list of proposal topics that connect to the novels your students have studied so that they are able to show their understanding of the novels in the context of the units of which the novels were a part.

Adapting the Call for Proposals with Different Classroom Texts

If your class studied *To Kill a Mockingbird, Their Eyes Were Watching God, The Catcher in the Rye*, and *Things Fall Apart*, your call for proposals could be:

1. Historical stories that convey the connections between apathy and inequity in the execution of justice
2. Complicated love stories that depict an individual's journey to self-revelation
3. Coming-of-age stories that capture the process of trying to make sense of a complicated society
4. International stories that examine the collision of traditional and colonizing cultures

Adapting the Project to a Unit Assessment Rather Than Final Assessment

If you do not have time at the end of the year to dedicate to this full-scale project because of other projects, exams, or pressures in your school community, you could use this project as an assessment at the end of one curricular unit. For example, if you finished a unit that included the study of *The Perks of Being a Wallflower*, you could adapt all of the requirements to focus on pitching a proposal to make this one novel into a film. This could serve as a competition between groups in one class because they would all be pitching the same idea. Even in this stripped-down form, the assessment empowers students to explain the relevance of a text and the importance of sharing it with a larger audience while also exercising their persuasive writing and public speaking skills.

Adapting the Project to a Writing Assessment without Public Speaking

If time at any point in the year is a pressure, you could also do this assessment without the public speaking element. The experience would be different in the sense that it would not challenge the students with a simulated real-life situation. However, it could still be valuable in allowing the students to express their understanding and knowledge of the curricular content using different kinds of writing skills.

6

Where Do *You* Go from Here?

High Stakes Does Not Equal High Standards

We have to acknowledge that for decades now, national politics has focused on assessment and, in particular, testing in light of the stark reality that our youth may not be measuring up academically to those in other industrialized countries. This has led to an increased pressure for standards and accountability that was most clearly articulated in George W. Bush's No Child Left Behind Act. Now, there is no denying that education has become a field overwhelmingly based on the results of standardized tests. It is difficult for any teacher, administrator, parent, or student to refute this, however we feel about it. Looking to test data for answers is easy, because that's what the majority seems to value. When local, state, or even the national government wants to gauge the success of schools, they have standardized tests to look to. The three major rationales for relying on standardized tests are that they are necessary within the increasingly globalized economy, they reduce educational inequality, and they increase assessment objectivity (Hursch 605). Many people believe that without standardized tests, standards for our students—what we expect them to be able to do—will be lowered (Hayden 610).

So, for many, the question is, why do something else? Here at East Side Community High School we feel that the answer, though complex in nature, is really simple: We want better for our students. We do not want our students to be known simply as a level on a state exam—we want them to be more, and we believe in the research and theories that argue alternative and authentic assessments lead to higher standards. This is not an issue that was neglected in the most recent national election. In their platform on education, President Obama and Vice President Biden stated, "This will include funds for states to implement a broader range of assessments that can evaluate higher-order skills, including students' abilities to use technology, conduct research, engage in scientific investigation, solve problems, and present and defend their ideas. These assessments provide immediate feedback so that teachers can begin improving student learning right away" (www.fairtest.org). We are not interested in preparing our students to succeed on exams; we are preparing them to hold their own in college classrooms.

As stated in the introduction, we firmly believe that our students are challenged by our curriculum based in authentic assessment tasks, and this allows them to succeed in life after high school as well as on the mandated tests. Because our curriculum and assessments hold students to high standards while equipping them with real-world skills, they are also equipped with the tools to succeed on high-stakes state tests. Grant Wiggins promotes the importance of authentic forms of assessment for students in *Educative Assessment: Designing Assessments to Inform and Improve Student Performance*. He stresses the importance of using assessment as a way to improve student learning and understanding of their own learning, while holding teachers accountable for providing rigorous and relevant instruction. In regard to standardized tests, he states that they "need only to show that the level of writing a student produces under these less than ideal circumstances correlates positively with his or her writing under better conditions" (321). The writing-as-a-product required by standardized tests has never been touted as a forum for students to display their best work. Rather, these pieces are "meant to be quickly used indicators of more complex performance. If the rigor and complexity of local work increase, then test scores are designed to increase. . . . [T]eachers need not teach worse in order to make test scores better" (Wiggins 320). This is at the heart of our belief in alternative, authentic forms of assessment. Teaching to the test may actually lower the level of instruction, as well as the depth of student learning. If we are only preparing students for the test, then we are only preparing them to successfully produce work that the "less than ideal circumstances" of the standardized tests require. These ideas are reflected in reputable, solid research of assessment:

> When well-constructed, normative assessments of accountability are linked to well-designed, curriculum-embedded instructional assessments, children perform better on accountability exams, but they do not because instruction has been narrowed to the specific content of the test. They do better on high-stakes tests because instruction can be targeted to the skills and needs of the learner using standards-based information the teacher gains from ongoing assessment and shares with the learner. (Meisels et al. 11)

We believe that if school-based assessments are authentic and offer alternatives to the high-stakes standardized tests, then students will be able to measure their success in a variety of ways and also score better on standardized tests.

What We Propose: A Start for Any School

In an ideal world, all schools would be able to create their own assessment tools to ensure that the high standards they have set for their students are being met. However, that would require much more systematic change than this book proposes. We suggest that if teachers in any school are creating authentic assessment practices that are connected to rigorous curriculum, then that teacher's students will also be prepared to achieve success on a standardized test. This is not an either/or situation. English teachers can create alternative assessments while still preparing students for the standardized reading and writing tests they have to pass.

Teachers and administrators may simply need to reorient the way they approach preparation for the standardized tests. "These new state and federal regulations have transferred power away from teachers, parents, and local community members and toward corporate and political leaders" (Hursch 605). To believe in authentic forms of assessment, however, is to believe in your school, teachers, and community and to hold yourself accountable for having high expectations and standards for all students. Even if teachers don't have to meet the demands of a standardized test, they are already under an obligation to ensure that they are holding their students to high standards through their assessments. The process of shifting toward alternative and authentic assessment from more traditional final exams or paper assignments will no doubt seem easier if you don't have to bow to the demands of standardized tests. But, even if standardized tests are a reality, as they are for most of us, the process can still be simple. It just requires a shift in thinking about how to approach the tests. Take a step back and ask yourself what skills students need to succeed on the test. Critical reading? Essay writing? Persuasion? Comparing texts? Literary vocabulary? These skills can and should be incorporated into any high school English curriculum. Students should demonstrate these skills on any form of assessment, formative or cumulative, traditional or alternative.

It is never an easy process to change from a more traditional structure to something new and different. This book is not intended to propose a full-scale restructuring or even provide lesson plans or assessments that can be duplicated as is and inserted into any classroom. East Side started with the portfolio-and-roundtable system, but that system has continued to evolve over the past decade and a half. Our philosophy on curriculum design and using the planning method outlined in Wiggins and McTighe's *Understanding by Design* is an even newer incorporation in our school.

The bottom line is that relevant curriculum and authentic assessment can be designed only within the context of your own school, which means it needs to be "site-base, locally controlled" (Huot 178). Our advice: start small and slow. If you are a teacher who wants to convince an administrator that this is a worthy option, design an authentic assessment for an existing unit. If you are reading *Their Eyes Were Watching God*, have the students take on the roles of different characters, research them and their relationships to the other characters, and create a talk show performance. Invite your administrator. The students will have to demonstrate their knowledge of the characters using evidence from the text and realistically explain their relationships with the other characters. The "host" and audience members will have to ask questions that show their understanding. A project like this does not have to be high stakes, but it can be a small step toward changing the priorities in your classroom culture and ultimately in your school culture.

Dealing with Time

Of course, one of the major constraints teachers and administrators feel around changes in curriculum is time. In the education system there never seems to be enough time, and this is often true because schools are dedicated to going beyond delivering the expected. There are ways to make time constraints less daunting, but again, it requires educators to rethink how they view time. Just as understanding why authentic and alternative forms of assessment are valid takes a shift in our approach to education, implementing authentic and alternative forms of assessment takes a shift in a school's approach to the daily schedule. The "trick is to make better use of available time" (Wiggins 314) and "challenging time-honored habits about the schedule. . . . [D]o all days have to follow the same schedule? Do all classes need to meet every day?" (Wiggins 316). The first step is to focus professional development time on curriculum design or redesign. The next step is to think about student schedules.

Though change seems difficult because it makes thing different, these innovations can work. They work at East Side, but they also have worked in entire districts and states. A case study of Connecticut shows how real progress was made by connecting teacher training to curriculum design and assessment. Teacher training is linked to the standards and curriculum design, with each district developing its own criteria for graduation that include but are not limited to a tenth-grade mastery test. Everything is more performance based and locally controlled but, most important, "student assessments are aimed at higher order thinking and performance skills embedded in state standards and are used to evaluate and continually improve practice" (Darling-Hammond 6).

One final consideration in making the shift toward authentic assessment and away from a sole emphasis on standardized tests is teacher pride and retention. Numerous studies have shown that teachers feel limited and frustrated by the "drill and kill," "one-size-fits-all" approach to teaching. With the focus on standardized tests and the narrowing of curriculum, teacher retention has been an enormous problem, much of it due to teachers' diminished sense of professionalism and ownership over their classrooms and the loss of teacher voices in decision-making processes (Perreault 705; Crocco and Costigan 514). To retain a sense of professionalism and pride in the field of education, we must ensure that teachers have a sense of ownership over both curriculum assessment in their classrooms, which will lead to greater teacher satisfaction and success and therefore higher retention.

We believe that students' journeys through English classes at East Side Community High School instill in them a love of reading, an ability to think critically, and a comfort and sense of empowerment that comes with knowing their voices matter and will be heard. At the end of the journey, they are true intellectuals who have met the challenges of our curriculum and our authentic assessments, who have achieved success on standardized tests, and who are prepared to be active learners in competitive college environments. This is our vision, one we constantly work toward, and it is our hope that this is a vision that can be shared in English classrooms across the country.

Appendix

Handout 1.1

Reading Conference Prep Sheet

*New/important work students must do before moving to next level

Benchmark Texts	*Shredderman; Wimpy Kid; Spiderwick*	*Bluford;* Mike Lupica, Beatrice Sparks; *Slam; Supernaturalist*	*Lightning Thief; Stargirl*	*Hunger Games; Push; Demonata; Immortal Instruments*
Levels	**(KLM) NOPQ**	**RST**	**UVW**	**XYZ**
Skills/ strategies/ artifacts	**KLM** **-Pacing and monitoring for meaning** *(Artifact: Sticky note at end of each chunk: What happened so far?)* ***What kind of a person is the character?** *(Artifact: Sticky note at end of chapter: Character is doing/saying ____ and this shows me she or he is ____.)* ***Characters don't change, but feelings do** **NOPQ** **-Characters change** *(Artifact: Sticky note at end of chapter: In the beginning my character was ____ but now my character is ______.)* ***Focus on character work: What kind of a person is the character? Clear character traits** *(Artifact: Sticky note at end of chapter: Trait and evidence OR RNB: Character trait/ evidence chart)* ***Character emotions** are explicit/clear, though reasons for emotions may not be obvious right away to reader or character ***Characters change** *(Artifact: Sticky note at end of chapter: What has changed and why/how did it change?)* ***Characters WANT things and have PROBLEMS** *(Artifact: RNB: Somebody/wanted/ but/so)* ***Small problems connected to a BIG problem; short-term solutions but big problem not always solved (at end of book); some are personal, some connected to character flaws** *(Artifact: RNB entry: What was the big problem? Did it get solved? Why or why not?)*	***Many characters that are there for a reason** *(Artifact: RNB: Character/traits/ importance chart)* ***Characters have many problems: Series of small, similar problems; big problem with many parts; internal vs. external problems** *(Artifact: RNB: Problem/ change chart)* ***We learn about characters through backstories (hard moments in the past that characters have experienced)** *(Artifact: Sticky note on backstory: What does this teach me about the character?* ***What lessons do characters learn? Solutions to problems teach lessons. (after reading in this band for a while)** *(Artifact: RNB entry)* *** Setting becomes important: What kind of place is this? Character's relationship to setting (can reflect character feeling)** *(Artifact: RNB or sticky note: What I know about this place.)*	***Characters face pressures that affect their behavior and choices** *(Artifact: RNB pressure map)* ***Deeper main character work:** **-unfold slowly** **-complicated/ conflicting emotions** **-backstory** *(Artifact: Sticky note: What new info have I learned about my character? OR RNB: Character/ traits/problem/change chart at end of book)* ***Relationships may not be stable** ***Reader knows more than character** *(Artifact: Sticky note: "I know . . . because . . .")* ***Reader must hold onto clues/info across big chunks of text** *(Artifact: Sticky note: "I know . . . I think it will be important because . . .")* ***What lessons do characters AND readers learn?** *(Artifact: RNB entry)* ***Series of problems** – not all resolved; some are connected to others or to places or other characters, some not; some solutions cause other problems ***Shifts in time or voice** ***Symbolism**	***Characters are often confused and under so much pressure; desires and motivations are unclear** *(Artifact: Somebody/ wanted/ but/ so chart)* ***Characters cause big change in environment and other characters' lives** *(Artifact: RNB reverse pressure map)* ***Setting is meaningful: symbolic, dangerous, new world with new rules for reader to learn** *(Artifact: Sticky note in front of book: What do we know about this place? OR RNB: What we know/ What effect it has on character chart)* ***Power matters; who has power? Why? What do they do with it?** *(Artifact: RNB entry)* ***Lessons are learned (implicit and explicit)** **What lessons do characters/readers learn about ourselves? The world?** *(Artifact: RNB entry)*

Handout 1.2

Ten Ways That Parents/Families Can Help Their Children Become Better Readers

East Side Community High School

1. Make sure that your child reads every single night for a minimum of 60 minutes.

- No exceptions.
- The best way to become a better reader is to read more.

2. Read as a family.

- Model reading.
- Read to or with your child.
- Have older children read to younger ones.
- Read the same books as your child.
- Create quiet space.
- Have set time.
- Establish family book clubs.

3. Ask your child about what she or he is reading and discuss the book or article with him or her

- What is the message or author's purpose?
- What does the book or article teach you? What is your evidence?
- What is happening "so far" in the book or article?
- What do you "predict" will happen next or later?
- What obstacle(s) do/does the main character face?
- What does the main character or person learn or accomplish?
- How is the character feeling? (Use words on the list.)

4. Have reading materials around the house and in child's room.

- Books
- Magazines

- Newspapers
- Build your child's library.
  - Visit bookstores/Strand (12th Street and Broadway–second floor).
  - Check out library discard sales.
  - Join Scholastic book club.
  - Give books and magazines as gifts.

5. Visit the library or bookstores with your child.
   - Use bookstores as libraries.
   - Make an afternoon of it.
   - Make sure everyone has library cards.

6. Encourage your child to learn and use new words.
   Learn new words from . . .
   - Reading
   - Television
   - Music
   - Movies
   - Advertisements and signs
   - Conversations
   - Sophisticated synonyms list

Own a dictionary and thesaurus that is age- and level-appropriate.

7. Find ways to integrate reading into other fun activities that interest your child.
   - Movies, music, television
   - Sports, cooking, and other hobbies
   - Travel and vacation

8. Track reading and establish incentives.
   - Set goals using "Reading Record" and "Reading Plan."
     - Nightly
     - Weekly
     - Number of books/Type of books

Handout 2.1

One Flew Over the Cuckoo's Nest Model Passage

Passage 1

The passage:
"She screamed when he grabbed for her and ripped her uniform all the way down the front. . . ." (p. 267)

Description of the passage:
This is the moment in the book when McMurphy attacks Nurse Ratched. Billy has just killed himself and Nurse Ratched blames McMurphy for his death. McMurphy refuses to accept this, and he breaks into the nurses' station, rips off her uniform, and chokes her. When the fight is over, McMurphy is sent to the Disturbed Ward and given a lobotomy.

Why this passage is significant:
I find this passage very troubling. As readers, we have been rooting for McMurphy since he entered the ward. We cheer him on as he gets the men to finally stand up to the nurse and reclaim their self-esteem. Billy's death stands as a clear reminder of the extent of the nurse's power over the men. Her attempt to blame McMurphy is unfair and wrong.

It makes sense that McMurphy would snap and attack the nurse. But, why does Ken Kesey have McMurphy rip off her clothes? As a woman, I cannot cheer when a man violates a woman's body. Perhaps Kesey is trying to reassert the dominance of a man's sexuality. Perhaps he is having McMurphy commit an act designed to most humiliate Nurse Ratched. What message is Kesey sending to readers? It is acceptable to violate a woman's body if she tries to emasculate men? In my opinion, Kesey is showing that men should never be ruled by a woman. However, it raises troubling questions about what Kesey believes is acceptable treatment of women.

Name____________________

Book____________________

Passage 1
The Passage:

Page number:

Description of the passage:

Why this passage is significant:

Handout 2.2

Questions: Strong and Weak

Examples of weak questions:
If you were Chief Bromden, would you have murdered McMurphy?
What does McMurphy do to Nurse Ratched?

What makes these weak questions?

Stronger questions:
Why might Ken Kesey have Bromden narrate the novel?
What purpose does the fishing trip serve in the novel?
In your opinion, does the book end on a hopeful note on the theme of society versus the individual?
Why does Kesey have McMurphy rip off the nurse's shirt, in addition to choking her?
What might that decision suggest about Kesey's views of gender roles and sexuality?

What makes these stronger questions?

As a group, please come up with two examples of strong questions for your novel

1.

2.

Example 2.1

Dear Book Lovers,

I am the twelfth-grade English teacher at East Side Community High School. This year we are launching a final project designed to have students demonstrate their proficiency in comprehending, analyzing, questioning, and discussing a work of literature.

The key component of this project is that each student will conduct an analytical discussion with an adult on the book. The students will be prepared with key passages, discussion questions, and thoughts on the author's purpose. The role of the adult is to engage with the student in a discussion of the book, much as you would with your peers in a book club. At the end of the conversation the adult will fill out a rubric and write brief comments on the discussion.

The student will be responsible for initiating the discussion, but you will need a copy of the book on hand as well as a reasonable familiarity with the text.

The students are reading one of the following books:

Breath, Eyes, Memory: Edwidge Danticat
Foxfire: Confessions of a Girl Gang: Joyce Carol Oates
A Lesson Before Dying: Ernest Gaines
The Secret Life of Bees: Sue Monk Kidd
Beasts of No Nation: Uzodinma Iweala
The Curious Incident of the Dog in the Night-Time: Mark Haddon
Catcher in the Rye: J. D. Salinger
The Kite Runner: Khaled Hosseini

If you have read, or would be willing to read, one of these books, we would love to have you facilitate a discussion! The discussions can be arranged at your convenience between May 29 and June 1 or June 4, 5, or 6. Each conversation will last between 30 and 40 minutes and can be scheduled any time between 8:30 a.m. and 3:30 p.m.

Please email me if you would be interested in participating!

Thanks,
Joanna Dolgin

Example 2.2

Sample Student Work: Jeremiah, *A Lesson Before Dying*

Passage 3: Chapter 29 is written as Jefferson's diary. In it he talks about a lot of things that are on his mind. This is a key moment in this book because we have never looked into the mind of Jefferson until now. This gives the reader an insight to his thoughts, and they are not negative at all.

" . . . Sometime mr wigin I just feel like telling you im like you but I don't kno how to say this cause I ain't never say it to nobody before an nobody ain't never say it to me."

This shows that Jefferson is a man, a man with feeling and not a "hog" as his lawyer put it. This shows that what Grant did for Jefferson actually worked. Before Jefferson was a hard-headed guy who didn't like anyone. He also let society make him who he was, but Grant came and changed all that. Grant made him into a man who expresses himself and isn't afraid to admit anything. Jefferson may not speak properly, but he dies with dignity.

Part B: Discussion Questions
*In your opinion do you think Grant is more of a man at the end of the book than in the beginning?

- After reading Jefferson's thoughts, he should feel a sense of accomplishment.
- Jefferson is the only person that makes Grant see what kind of person he really was and all the people who do love him.

*What is the main symbol in the book? Is it the chair or Jefferson's diary?

- To me, Jefferson's diary is more of a symbol because it shows who Jefferson can be once someone believed in him.
- The chair was made to strike fear into the hearts of the people who were on the scene where Jefferson was going to die. It shows the power of the system.

Part C: Author's Purpose
There are many reasons the author may have wanted to write this book. Manhood is the main theme in this book. You have people that have different views of what qualities a real man should have. Just because a man is educated doesn't mean he's a real man, according to the reverend. The author used the situation with Grant and Jefferson to show people that even men need another person to become a man. Without Jefferson, Grant would not have found himself at the end of the book. The author's main purpose was to show readers that it takes more to be a man than meets the eye. Just because you advance yourself in certain areas doesn't make you more of a man.

Example 2.3

Figure 10.

- prepared
- confident
- expressive
- enthusiastic
- secure
- convincing
- believable

East Side Community High School Independent Reading Final Project

Student Jeremiah Book 2 Evaluator Sayeeda Carter

Please take some notes on the conversation: (key ideas the student presents, questions)

- caught his interest becaause of his history class topics / paying attention to various historical differences
- opened his mind to what a man is? — (not only education)
- opinion of Grant — (lost except w/ regards to Vivian and his love for her)
- sees Jefferson due to Vivian's influence
  Grant hasn't found his purpose
  — Both Jefferson & Grant are receiving a lesson

what about the style of E.J. Gaines interested you?

How would author define manhood.

education vs intelligence —

how Jefferson grows emotionally, accepts help.

- making Jefferson to a man

Grant ⟷ Jefferson what qualities do they get from each other

"Made Grant be a person who won't give up."

excellent Discussion questions

fantastic discussion around two pivitol symbols — the chair vs notebook

TODAY

- life is about choice — intelligence vs education
  used novel & made connection to Bible.

* tradition, family values, Society making people lazy

what qualities MAKE a man — what is E.J. Gaines definition of a man?

- determined
- Know himself
- opthmistic

- climax (2)
- literally
- protagonist
- narrator
- hook

perspective

94

	Excellent	Good	Fair	Needs Improvement
Analysis	Sophisticated analysis, demonstrating in-depth understanding of selected passages and the themes in the text	Presents a thoughtful understanding of passage's significance with some in-depth analysis	Presents a basic understanding of selected passages with limited analysis	Shows limited understanding of passage's significance
Discussion questions	Questions got to key issues, were thoughtful, and prompted discussion	Questions were open-ended and prompted discussion	Questions prompted some discussion	Questions were basic and the student's opinions poorly developed
Evidence	Student was able to support all opinions with relevant evidence	Student was able to support most opinions with relevant evidence	Student had a limited ability to support ideas with evidence	Student was unable to support ideas with evidence
Author's purpose	Student had a deep understanding of author's purpose	Student presented a well thought out understanding of author's purpose	Student had some sense of author's purpose	Student lacked a clear sense of author's purpose
Familiarity	Student knew the book backwards and forward	Student is very familiar with characters, themes, and key events	Student struggled to remember certain characters, themes, events	Student was unable to recall significant characters, themes, events
Presentation	Student was poised. Student started the conversation with ease. Student was extremely well prepared	Student carried him/herself well. Started the conversation with ease. Student was well prepared	Student's poise faltered at times. Student had difficulty beginning the conversation. Student was prepared	Student lacked poise. Student was unable to begin the discussion. Student lacked preparation

FEEDBACK: Please offer some positive feedback and make suggestions on areas where the student needs improvement.

fantastic – will debrief in person

Handout 3.1

Roundtable Agenda

One adult at each table will be the group leader. Please hand out rubrics and make sure they are filled out by every group member for each presentation. This is the suggested time frame to ensure that each student gets the same amount of time to present. (Approximately 35 minutes per student)

- Cover Letter (5 minutes)
  Each group member should receive a copy of the presenter's cover letter. The student will read the letter aloud as others follow along on the page.

- Show Work to Group (5 minutes)
  Each group member should receive samples of the presenter's work from this semester. Please rotate the work every few minutes. Below are the materials students should have:

Reading Folder Readers Notebook Writers Notebook Writing Folder History Folder Work Folder(with exhibition pieces)

- Share Independent Reading Work (5 minutes)
  Students should share reading rubrics and Books I've Read This Year chart.

- Mini-lesson (5 minutes)
  Lesson, poster, and activity about a specific skill that the student has learned.

- Guest Questions (10 minutes)
  Refer to questions and terms page to get started. You can also ask your own questions.

- Fill out presentation rubric (5 minutes)
  Finish by filling out the presentation rubric form.

Handout 3.2

Name of Student: ______________________________

Name of Evaluator: ______________________________

6th Grade Humanities Roundtable—June 2007

Presentation Rubric

Please fill in the following box while you are reading the student presenter's cover letter and looking through her or his portfolio. These comments will be shared with the student later.

I noticed . . .   *I wonder . . .*   *I liked . . .*

You will need to evaluate the student presenter on three categories. Each category counts as one out of five points. The points are:

5= Excellent 4=Good 3=Satisfactory 2=Needs Work 1=Unsatisfactory

Category:

1. Cover Letter

- ➢ **Student typed her or his cover letter.**

  5 4 3 2 1

- ➢ **Cover letter includes seven paragraphs that show thoughtful reflection of content or skills learned.**

  5 4 3 2 1

- ➢ **Student edited for spelling, punctuation, and grammar.**

  5 4 3 2 1

2. Presentations and Discussion

- Student was prepared with documentation about her or his reading work (notebook & reading records).

  5 4 3 2 1

- Student was prepared with a presentation about a skill or subject we studied this year (poster).

  5 4 3 2 1

- Student participated in the group discussion and answered questions with evidence.

  5 4 3 2 1

- Student was focused and respectful during other group members' presentations.

  5 4 3 2 1

- Student asked questions of others.

  5 4 3 2 1

Handout 3.3

Roundtables

Guest Questions

Here are some questions you might want to ask the students:

Reading	Writing
How do you know if your reading has improved?	How do you find powerful subjects to inspire mystery stories?
How do you learn about a character in a book you are reading?	How do myths work?
How can you track the changes a character goes through?	What are myths?
How do you know the theme of a book?	How do you make powerful decisions as a writer?
How do you recognize significant details?	How do you know your revision skills have improved?
How do you talk with your book group in a powerful way?	Did working with a writing partner help you? Explain why or why not.
How do you use sticky notes to remind you what to discuss with your group?	How do you add specific and significant details or evidence to improve your writing?
What does it mean to be a powerful reader?	How do you grab your reader's attention from the very beginning of your writing?
Which genre (e.g., mystery, mythology, realistic fiction) did you most enjoy reading this semester? Why?	How do you know when your writing is ready to publish?
How have you struggled as a reader?	How did you use the writing cycle? Did it help improve your writing?
What are your major accomplishments as a reader? Why are you proud of this?	Why is it important for you to be a powerful writer?

You could also ask students about their work habits, such as attendance, homework, organization, quality of work, and taking initiative.

Handout 3.4

Sixth-Grade Humanities Portfolio

Cover Letter

You will need to have a letter to present at your humanities roundtables. It will explain what you have done and learned at East Side this semester.

You should organize your letter by following these guidelines:

Dear Reader,

Paragraph #1: Introduction

- A hook
- Your name, age, and grade
- What was your favorite unit that you studied this semester? (Ex.: *Holes*, Mystery, Mythology). Explain how it changed you as a reader or writer.

Paragraph #2: Independent Reading

- What makes you a powerful reader?
- How many books have you read this semester?
- How much reading do you do outside of class? Where and when do you read?
- How do you record your reading?
- Which two books did you like best this semester? Explain why.
- What kinds of books can you read now that you didn't read before?

Paragraph #3: *Holes* (by Louis Sachar)

- What did you enjoy most about reading *Holes*?
- Which *Holes* mini-lesson helped you grow most as a reader? (Ex.: foreshadowing, flashbacks, story lines, time lines)
- How did readers theater help you to enjoy and understand *Holes*?
- What is powerful about reading a whole book together as a reading community?

- How did writing two essays about *Holes* help you to understand the book better?
- Why is it important to use evidence from a book (quote the text) when you write an essay?

Paragraph #4: Mystery

- What was the best mystery book that you read?
- Explain your experience with participating in a book club. What did you learn about yourself?
- Compare reading alone to reading with a book club. Reflect on which way works better for you as a reader.
- How did making a poster with your group help you to understand your mystery books?
- What do mystery writers need to include in their stories to make them suspenseful?
- What was your process in writing your mystery story?
- How did working with a writing partner help you to revise?
- Are you a successful mystery writer? How do you know?

Paragraph #5: Mythology

- Who was your favorite goddess or god? Explain why.
- How did making a poster with your partner help you to appreciate your goddess or god better?
- What do mythology writers need to include in their stories to make them powerful?
- What was your process in writing your myth?
- How did working with a writing partner help you to revise?
- Are you a successful mythology writer? How do you know?

Paragraph #6: Writing Workshop

- How do you know that you have grown as a writer since arriving at East Side?
- What has been the most important part of the writing cycle for you this semester? (Ex.: planning, drafting, revising, editing, proofreading, or publishing)

- What do powerful writers make sure they do before handing in a final draft?
- What is the difference between an essay and a story?
- What is your favorite piece of writing that you have done this semester? Explain why it is powerful.

Paragraph #7: Writing Essays

- What is an essay, and why do people write them?
- How is an essay organized? (Ex.: amount and kinds of paragraphs)
- What is a thesis (bold statement)?
- What do you need to mention in the introduction?
- Why do examples and evidence in the body paragraphs make your essay stronger?
- Why do good writers include quotes in a literary essay?
- Why do you need to repeat the same information from the introduction in the conclusion?

Paragraph #8: Writing Stories (Mystery and Myth)

- What is story?
- What are some strategies you can use to help you make up a story?
- What kinds of details do you need to add to your stories to make them powerful? (Ex.: lead, setting, dialogue, character traits, actions, onomatopoeia)

Paragraph #9: Conclusion

- What advice about humanities class would you give an incoming sixth grader?
- Describe the most important thing you have learned this semester.
- How have you grown as a learner since arriving at East Side?
- Describe two behavior strategies that helped you focus and become a better student in humanities class.
- Which of the habits of work have you improved on this semester? (Ex.: attendance, homework, organization, quality, taking initiative)
- Which of the habits of work do you want to improve next semester?
- What are your reading and writing goals for seventh grade?
- What are you planning to do this summer to make sure you don't forget what you learned in sixth grade?

Sincerely,
(Your Full Name)

Example 3.1

Johnny Collado's Cover Letter

Johnny Collado
6/11/09
Humanities

"Everybody handed their project in already!" said Sarvenaz.

"But, I can't!" I said

"Why!?!"

When I first got to seventh grade I depended on the teacher to hold my hand and guide me through all projects step by step. I worked at a slow pace and hardly got my work in. But one day Sarvenaz said, "I can't always be there to help you step by step. I have a whole class to teach; you need to be more independent."

"Okay, I understand." I said to Sarvenaz. She told me the training wheels come off in seventh grade and it's time to be more independent, so I took her advice. From then on I worked by myself and I got faster. I got my work done on time, I handed in work when I had to, and I did it by myself. This year I became more independent.

"Okay, stop and jot, make sure to fill in the whole box." Sarvenaz said. For history we used to write in thought boxes to explain what we think about in history in order to prepare for our discussions. And we would have to read what was on our paper to our partner. But as we became better thinkers, we wrote our thoughts freely and we wrote more than just what can fit in boxes. Now our discussions have more deep thinking. This makes me more powerful as a thinker, and I think it's great.

When I got to seventh grade I was still reading at a sixth grade level. As I go on to higher grades I want to be on the level I need to be on. So I want to read hard and challenging books over the summer and next year so I can become a better reader.

Thank you for coming to my roundtables,
Johnny Collado

Example 3.2

Eloiza Miranda
Block 1/7
June 12, 2009

Humanities—Cover Letter

"OMG! I don't feel like reading! What's the point?" When I first came to humanities I did not like reading because I thought it was boring, but now I realized I haven't been picking the right books in genre so the librarian Andrea helped me find books that I really liked, for example, poetry, mystery, and anecdotes.

My skills are getting better because I found something that I love to read. What got my interest is that I will love to do more is Book Clubs. I was in a book club with Mesha, Kimberly, and Jet. It was fun because when I don't understand something, they helped me understand it. Another thing that's great about book clubs is you have someone to share your thoughts and ideas with. It makes me more independent.

I am not a bad student in humanities. I don't disrespect the teacher because when I met Sarvenaz, she was strict, but she's a really nice teacher. I think her being strict was the right thing to do because she pushed me to be a better reader and writer. She did not let me give up, and that's why I'm so good in humanities.

I live in the Lower East Side, and there's a lot of violence, gun shots, and fires. But you know what? I'm no part of that. I believe that I can be educated and go to college, have a career and be successful so I don't end up on the streets getting shot.

Example 3.3

June Cover Letter—Victor Sanchez

"Nice work, Victor," said my teacher Sarvenaz when I first got to the seventh grade. I didn't know much, but I was always doing my work or doing what I'm supposed to do. During the lessons and teachings of Sarvenaz, I knew more and more. But I was not doing work much. I was always talking in class with my friends. I think that's when I started to know more people. I got distracted so I didn't do my work or do what I'm supposed to do. What I learned about being a good kid is you can always have time to chill or to talk with your friends outside of class.

In the middle of the year Sarvenaz started to do history. I never really liked history. To me it is so boring and I thought why listen if I already got history with Howard. Then we started to watch a movie called Roots. I really liked it. We had to stop and jot every time she would stop the movie. That movie taught the history of what Sarvenz was trying to teach me.

Later on in the year we started to read a book called Nightjohn. Every time Sarvenaz finished a chapter, she would let us talk without her interfering. That really got me interested in the book. It was good that she was not in it because it let us know that you know that you don't always have to count on the teacher. It got me interested because every time the students would say something that I didn't agree with, I would jump in the conversation so the students can hear what I think about what they said.

You know, it's funny that in the beginning of the year I'm good. In the middle of the year I'm bad. Then I work my butt off again so I can get a good grade because of all the bullshit I did in the middle of the year. So I guess my goal for next year is to be a leader not a follower. I want to be a leader and do my work because at the end it all pays off and you get the grades you deserve for all the hard work you did during the whole year.

Handout 3.5

Roundtables

Prove You Learned It!

Goal: Pick something that you struggled with at the beginning of the year but later learned how to do. Make a poster to prove that you've mastered it. Here are some options:

Reading	Writing
How do I know if my reading has improved?	How do I prove my thesis in an essay?
How do I have a discussion with my book group in a powerful way?	How do I make powerful revisions as a writer?
How do I learn about my character?	How does working with a partner improve my writing?
How can I track the changes a character goes through?	How do I add specific and significant details or evidence to improve my writing?
How do I know the theme of a book?	How do I grab my reader's attention from the very beginning of my writing?
What does it mean to be a powerful reader?	

How Do I Build a Poster?

Step 1: Write down the question that you're going to answer on your planning paper.

Step 2: Find evidence in your notebooks and folders that answer the question. You need two or three different pieces of your work from both first semester and second semester.

Step 3: Explain how each piece of evidence proves that you mastered the skill. The improvement should be really obvious.

Step 4: Clearly answer the question that you chose.

Step 5: Once your teacher approves your plan, make a poster including all the above information for everyone to see.

Example 3.4

420 East 12th Street
New York, N.Y. 10009
Tel: (212) 460-8467
Fax: (212) 260-9657
Principal: Mark Federman

June 11, 2007

Dear Families and Friends,

I would like to invite you to participate in your child's humanities portfolio roundtable on **Thursday, June 21**. On that day, students will be presenting their work to a small committee, which will include students, staff, and outside guests . . . **hopefully you can be one of those guests!** This is an opportunity to help evaluate and celebrate student work. The roundtables can work only with the help of adults to look at student work, listen to student presentations, ask questions, and participate in discussions.

Please fill in the form below letting me know whether or not you will be able to join us for this event. Your child's roundtable will be held on **June 21 from 8:30–10:30**. Please let me know if you will be able to attend the humanities roundtable by checking off the sheet below and having your child return it to school immediately.

Thank you very much.

Yours,
Sarvenaz Zelkha
Sixth-grade humanities teacher
(347-512-0408)

Student's Name: ______________________________

Family/Friend's Name: ________________________

Contact Phone Number for Family/Friend: ____________________________

______ Yes, I will attend the roundtable on June 21 from 8:30–10:30.

______ No, I will not attend the roundtable on June 21 from 8:30–10:30.

Parent Signature_________________________

Handout 4.1

Twelfth-Grade English: First Semester Cover Letter
Due Thursday, January 22
*****If you do not submit a typed, proofread draft by Thursday, January 22, you will not be allowed to present at the roundtable!*****

Introduction

- In your opinion, why do people read tragedies?
- What texts have we studied this semester?
- What types of assignments are in your portfolio?

Section 1: Tragedy

- Which tragedy that we've read best captures human nature? Explain.
- Considering what you know about Aristotle's definition of a tragic hero, how would you define a tragic hero?
- Explain which character you think is the most tragic, tragic hero: Oedipus, Antigone, Creon, Othello, Eddie, or Laramie. Defend that choice!

Section 2: Important Texts
Choose one of the books or plays you have read this semester that you think is important for other people to read. (It may be something you read during independent reading, or one of the five tragedies we read as a class.)

- Include the title, author, and a brief summary of the text you have chosen.
- Why is it an important text?
- What can people learn from reading this text?
- Choose one passage from the text that you think is key and explain its significance.

Section 3: Independent Reading

- Choose one of the best books you've read this year and briefly explain the plot and why you enjoyed it. Be sure to include the title and author.
- How many books have you COMPLETED this semester? Explain how you are able to read the amount that you do.

Section 4: You as an English Student

- How have you grown as a reader and writer this semester?
- Which assignment or kind of assignment (e.g., essay, personal narrative, creative writing, acting out a scene, test) was the most important for you? Why?
- How will you improve next semester?

Handout 4.2

Name: ______________________________

High School English Matrix

	Ninth Grade	Tenth Grade	Eleventh Grade	Twelfth Grade
Narrative (anecdote, vignette, memoir, college essay) (3)	**(1)**	**(1)**		(1)
Essay (persuasive, literary, personal, comparative) (6)	**(1)**	**(1)**	**(2)**	(2)
Creative Writing (poetry, fiction, playwriting, historical fiction)(3)	**(1)**	(1)	(1)	
Public Speaking and/or Documents (speech, debate, performance, reviews, etc.) (5)	**(1)**	**(1)**	**(2)**	**(1)**
Independent Reading (books completed lists)	o Minimum 40 books completed	o Minimum 35 books completed	o Minimum 25 books completed	o Minimum 25 books completed
Roundtables and Cover Letters (4)	**(1)**	**(1)**	**(1)**	**(1)**
Honors Status	___ **Honors** **(90% or above on all)**	___ **Honors** **(90% or above on all)**	___ **Honors** **(90% or above on all)**	___ **Honors** **(90% or above on all)**

Handout 4.3

Roundtable Debate
Which Tragic Hero Is the Most Tragic?

You and your partner will engage in a debate over whose tragic hero is the most tragic.

The Format

Assertion 1: Three minutes
The first student will present his arguments supporting why his tragic hero is the most tragic. He will use at least one direct quote. He may use more.

Question 1: Three minutes
Student 2 will ask questions that Student 1 must answer.

Assertion 2: Three minutes
Student 2 will present her arguments supporting why her hero is the most tragic. She will use at least one direct quote. She may use more.

Question 2: Three minutes
Student 1 will ask questions that Student 2 must answer.

Closing Statement 1: One minute
Student 1 will make his final arguments.

Closing Statement 2: One minute
Student 2 will make her final arguments.

At this time the guest may ask questions of both students.

Some issues to consider:

- Aristotle's definition of a tragic hero.
- Is dying more tragic than surviving?
- Is suicide more tragic than murder?
- The smaller the flaw, the greater the tragedy?
- The greater the epiphany, the greater the tragedy?

You must be able to define and explain how each applies to your character:

- Aristotle's view of a tragic hero
- Flaw (Hamartia)
- Epiphany

Goals of this debate:

- Defend your ideas with evidence.
- Understand and provide a counterargument to an alternative perspective.
- Demonstrate your understanding of two of the texts we read this semester.
- Make connections between books.
- Take effective notes to enhance your argument.

Example 4.1

Elizabeth V. January 26, 2009

Tragic Hero Debate

*****Creon** is the most tragic, tragic hero of all five plays.

- **High Stature**—King of Thebes
- He is a **good leader but not perfect**. Wants the best for his people, does not think anyone should get special treatment because state laws are the most important because they keep order.
- **Scared** that if he does not punish Antigone, then the city will be destroyed because others will follow in her footsteps by breaking the state laws.

  > Anarchy, anarchy! Show me a greater evil! This is why cities tumble and the great houses rain down this is what scatters armies. (Act 1.2.42)

- His **tragic flaw** is that he is too focused on being a tough leader but is not wise. His hubris gets in the way of his willingness to compromise. Sometimes good leaders need to compromise for the sake of the people.

  > As long as I am king, no traitor is going to be honored with the loyal man. But whoever shows by word and deed that he is on the side of the state, he shall have my respect when he is living and my reverence when he is dead. (Act 1.1.44)

- His **epiphany** comes toward the end. He realizes that he will lose his family and the support from the people of Thebes if he proceeds with the decision he has made to punish Antigone.
- His **punishment does exceed the "moral crime"** he committed. Creon loses everyone he loves and is not able to correct his wrongs when he tries to free Antigone. He is left alive which is even worse than death because he is left alone and he lives with the burden of his family's death.

Closing argument: Creon is the most tragic hero because he perfectly fits Aristotle's definition of a tragic hero. He clearly realizes that what he was doing was wrong, and he is the only tragic hero who tries to fix his mistake.

Handout 4.4

DIRECTIONS FOR STUDENTS AND VISITORS

Welcome to the Twelfth-Grade English Portfolio Roundtables. Thank you for attending! The purpose of this roundtable is to provide a forum for students to reflect on and discuss what they have accomplished and learned in their study of English this semester. Students should be prepared to defend their ideas and must be held accountable for the quality of their work and reflection. Please follow the directions below for each presenting student.

1. **Reading Student Cover Letter and Reviewing Student Portfolio (10 minutes):** Participants read cover letter to themselves. After reading the cover letter, participants closely examine the work inside the student's portfolio.

   Record on the evaluation sheet comments and questions for the student generated by what you read in the cover letter and observe in the portfolio. These questions will help stimulate dialogue in the next section of the roundtable.

2. **Dialogue (12 minutes):** All participants (adults and peers) ask the presenting student questions raised by the cover letter and the work in the portfolio. Questions can relate to the content of the course, specific assignments, issues raised in the cover letter, and the student's learning process and growth. Questions may be addressed to all students at the roundtable to facilitate a group discussion. Please consult the essential questions and discussion ideas sheet for suggestions. Please avoid questions on what makes a tragic hero, as that will be the content of the debate.

3. **Repeat steps 1 and 2 for the second and third students.**

4. **Debate (15 minutes):** All students will engage in a debate on the question, "Who is the most tragic hero?" Student 1 will present a three-minute speech on why her hero is the most tragic. Students 2 and 3 will then have two minutes to ask challenging questions. Student 2 will then have three minutes to give his speech, and Students 1 and 3 will have two minutes for questions. (Repeat for Student 3 when necessary!) Each student should then spend one minute offering a concluding statement.

5. **Assessment and Sharing of Feedback (5 minutes):** Please use the evaluation sheet to evaluate the cover letter and presentation of each student. Participants are encouraged to share feedback with students verbally and/or allow students to read over completed evaluation sheets.

STUDENTS: Please put all evaluation sheets in the designated folder at the front of the room, NOT back in your portfolio. ALSO give Joanna a copy of your final cover letter.

Handout 4.5

Twelfth-Grade English Roundtable
Evaluator Name:______________________
Student Presenting:_____________________________

Part 1: Cover Letter and Portfolio

	Comments/Questions on Cover Letter/Portfolio:
Demonstrated Understanding of Content: 1 2 3 4 5 Overall Quality of Writing: 1 2 3 4 5 Presents honest, insightful reflection about learning process and growth: 1 2 3 4 5	

Part 2: Responses to Discussion Questions

Expert	Practitioner	Apprentice	Novice
Thoroughly and clearly demonstrated understanding of different units *Fluently* used sophisticated language and ideas to analyze themes and make connections between texts	Clear and competent demonstration of understanding of most units Able to offer basic analysis or limited connections between texts	*Partially* able to demonstrate understanding of only some units or ideas Needed help to clearly explain concepts or make connections	Needed a level of support in providing answers that shows they did not yet have sufficient understanding in the themes of this course

Part 3: Debate

Expert	Practitioner	Apprentice	Novice
_*Thoroughly* and clearly explained why character is most tragic _*Thoroughly* prepared with points and evidence _*Actively* took notes in response to others _*Fluently* and convincingly responded to questions and ideas presented by others	_Clear explanation showing understanding of tragic hero and character _Competent preparation, may have stumbled at times _Took limited notes _Answered questions posed by others	_*Partially* explained character in connection to tragic hero _*Partially* prepared or needed help from others _*Unable* to answer questions clearly or pose clear questions to others	_Not able to explain why character was most tragic OR UNPREPARED

OVERALL EVALUATION (Please circle one)

EXPERT **PRACTITIONER** **APPRENTICE** **NOVICE**

Additional Comments:

Handout 4.6

Twelfth-Grade English Roundtables
Essential Questions and Discussion Ideas

Unit 1: The Personal Essay

- How do you convey a powerful moment in writing?
- What makes a strong personal essay?
- How did you select your topic?
- How does the writing process enhance the final product?

Unit 2: Greek Tragedy (*Oedipus Rex* and *Antigone*)

- Do we control our destinies?
- Is Oedipus his own worst enemy or a victim of fate?
- Why does Oedipus blind himself at the end of the play? How does Sophocles use the imagery of sight and blindness throughout the play?
- How did ideas around gender roles cause the tragedy in *Antigone?*
- Who better fits Aristotle's definition of a tragic hero: Antigone or Creon?
- What can *Grey's Anatomy* teach us about tragic heroes?

Unit 3: Shakespeare (*Othello*)

- Why is Shakespeare still read today?
- Who (or what) is to blame for Desdemona's death?
- How does racism contribute to the tragedy of the play?
- How did working with the actors from the Shakespeare Society enhance your understanding of the play?
- In your opinion, why does Shakespeare choose to have Iago live at the end of the play?
- In your opinion, does Othello regain his dignity at the end of the play?

Unit 4: Modern Tragedies (*A View from the Bridge* and *The Laramie Project*)

- What themes do modern tragedies share with ancient tragedies?
- How do notions of masculinity influence the tragedy in *A View from the Bridge?*
- Why does Eddie kiss both Catherine and Rodolpho?
- Why does Alfieri say that Eddie is a hero for "refusing to settle for half"? What does that mean?
- Why does Arthur Miller have Eddie's dying words be, "My B"? What does this show us about Eddie?
- Define and explain the difference between homophobia, tolerance, and acceptance. How would you classify the town of Laramie?
- Does Laramie have an epiphany?
- Does the philosophy of "Live and Let Live" cause Matthew's death?
- Is Laramie an allegory for American society?
- Why does Dennis Shepard spare the life of Aaron McKinney?
- What does hate do to people?

Independent Reading

- How are you able to read the amount that you do?
- What genres do you prefer to read and why?
- Why does East Side devote so much time to independent reading?

Example 4.2

8th grade June 2005

Dear Reader,

Hey people! Know what time it is? It's time for cover letters! Hi! My name is Nazia. I'm in the 8th grade. This is my second year at East Side. This year I've grown as a student because I care more about homework and class work. I care about my grades more. The purpose in writing a cover letter is to tell you what we did throughout the semester, our strength, goals, and weaknesses. This year what stood out to me was that last year instead of responding to our book in class, we were allowed to do it at home, which gave us more time to thoroughly think about the book.

To be a powerful reader is to be able to like reading and reading books that are different, such as longer books or different genres. This year I read 27 books. Three of my favorite books this year were *Shredderman 1*, *Shredderman 2*, and *Shredderman 3* all by Wendalin Van Draanan. I found these books humorous, mysterious, and nail biting. I choose books by the cover, title, genres, blurbs, and how long it is. That always works because I choose books that I think are going to be funny.

Two reading strategies I find useful from my reader's notebook are inferring and the messages. Inferring is when you read between lines and to make a guess. One time I was inferring was in the story *The Good Girls*. I inferred that he drank too much, and he was completely passed out. A message is what a book is trying to teach you. The message in the book *Lost and Found* was that sometimes people do bad things and that changes their lives. What makes an excellent book talk is speaking out loud, giving a good explanation about what the story is about, and discussing the message, characters, setting, etc. Jessica's book talk was very good. She explained her book and didn't tell us what happened at the end. She spoke out loud and gave reasons why the book was good. I've grown as a reader because I read more at home and I choose books from different kinds of genres instead of the same genres.

A story structure is the problem in the story, the rising action, climax, the falling action, and the resolution. One story our class read was *Oliver Button* by Tomie dePaola. The problem in the story was that Oliver was called a sissy because he liked activities that girls usually do. The rising action was when some kids wrote on the wall that Oliver Button is a sissy. The climax was when Oliver was going to perform. The falling action was when he performed on stage and everyone clapped. The resolution was when Oliver read on the wall that Oliver is a STAR! The message of the story was that don't judge someone by what they do, judge someone by how they do it. The most important thing I've learned about reading short stories is that you don't read the text only, you also read between the lines. (Subtext)

For writing a powerful editorial you have to do many things. First, plan it, then revise it to look for assertions, evidence, or a thesis, and a conclusion. It also has to have five paragraphs. An intro, three body paragraphs, and a conclusion. My second editorial, *It's not fair,* was not the best thing ever on the first draft. It didn't have assertions. On the final draft I had everything my essay needed. So I got an A-. I supported my thesis with evidence by making sure I had something that has to do with my thesis. The most important thing I learned about writing essays is that the essay always has to have a thesis, and that's what the essay has to support. I've grown as a writer because on my first editorial I got a C- and on my second one I got an A-!

The most important thing I learned in humanities was in writing because last year my writing used to be very poor, but now I can write very good essays. A habit of work I am proud of is organization and time. I am almost always organized and always bring in my work on time. Something I work on is initiative. I don't go to after school, or sometimes revise my work. So I need to work on that. My class has grown in many ways because in the beginning of the school year, we didn't really work as a team. But now we work as a group and help each other.

Sincerely,
Nazia K.

9th Grade

Dear Reader,

I am curled up on the right side of the couch, lost in *Totally Joe*. I am almost finished, but it's really late and my mom says go to sleep. My temper is rising, but I just go to bed. But then I get back up from my bed and I look to see where she is. YES! She's in the kitchen. I go to my book bag and get my book, and somehow my mom sees me. I see her opening the drawer for something. OH CRAP!!! She has a spatula!!!! So I run through the hallway and finally she catches me. So I just give up and go back to bed. I don't know why, but I just couldn't put the book down. Every page had a special thing in it. I just can't explain it.

Since September I have read 43 books. My favorite book this year was *The Burn Journals* by Brent Runyon. *The Burn Journals* by Brent Runyon is a memoir. It was about a boy who attempted to commit suicide. I also liked it because he was a teenager and he wrote the book as if he's still a teenager. He wrote what was really in his mind. The right book is when it has a good blurb, a good cover, and a good title.

To support my inferences I used quotes from the books I was reading. In my reader's notebook I would write about *Esperanza Rising* by Pam Munoz Ryan. In my notebook I was taking out some quotes from the book about her mom's decision. I inferred that Esperanza's mom will run away from Esperanza's uncle since he wanted to marry her. He had asked her to marry him on page 31. He made a deal with her. He asked her if she wanted, she could still be rich. She said she'll think about marrying him. But she didn't, she ran away. I noticed that when I pick books, they're mostly fictional books. I pick books that are about teen issues. I was reading *Pictures of Hollis Woods* by Patricia Reilly Giff. Hollis was a foster child who would always run away from her foster parents. But the recent foster parents are so nice to her. And she hates to say it, but she likes them and wants to live with them forever. But she is to leave their house for some reason. She never used to have confidence in herself. I know this because in the book she said ". . . I looked different . . . almost pretty" (32). This means that before she used to think that she wasn't pretty.

Good readers read a lot and understand what they are reading. They choose books that will challenge them. Good readers infer a lot while they're reading their books. Inferring is when readers create interpretation to enrich and deepen their experience in a text. They guess why things happen. Readers infer about character traits, relationship, roles, forces and pressures, and choices. Sometimes inferring involves predicting. Readers infer to know what will probably happen in the future. Another thing a good reader does is makes text-text connections. Text-text connections are when you have an idea of how the text is going to be structured and what it's going to sound like. You comment on what you know about the author in order to understand the text better. A good reader also asks questions. They are questioning the text. They question their text and hope to get the answers to their questions. They ask questions to make inferences, to understand an author's style, to locate a specific answer in a text, and to consider. They also synthesize. To synthesize you have to recognize the patterns in the text and you have to give your opinion. I would say I'm a pretty good reader because I read every day, and I do make connections, I question what I read, and I infer. Like this one time I was reading *The Burn Journals*. I was making a text-to-world connection to a person I knew. He wanted to commit suicide because of stress. In *The Burn Journals*, Brent wanted to commit suicide so he set himself on fire, but was fortunately saved. In the book *Totally Joe*, I inferred that Joe's ex-boyfriend was going to break up with him because he doesn't like people thinking that he's gay, even though he is. My inference turned out to be true. There was this one time I was reading *The Body of Christopher Creed* by Carol Plum Ucci. And there was this point where I got really confused. And I started to question what one of the character had said. Since this was in the eighth grade, I asked my humanities teacher, Elisa, what she thought it meant, and it meant something so different. Well, this shows that questioning the text can sometimes lead you to answers and less confusion. *Blood and Chocolate* by Annette Curtis Klause, I synthesized that the girl that was the main character goes back to her flashback then back to the present.

My writing has improved by using dialogue, by staying in the moment, and cutting out unnecessary words. In my anecdote, I remember when I first wrote it. It had so many things that didn't belong there. I had to erase a whole paragraph because it had nothing to do with that moment. It was supposed to be about that moment, and I went back to the past. So I had to cut out the whole thing. I used dialogue and that's what makes it seem like it was really that moment I was talking about.

The most effective piece of work I did was my memoir. While writing it I started out with five pages, but I know no one would actually read five pages. So I had to take out a lot of things. I had to go through two drafts, but those two drafts had a lot of editing. I had to revise it so many times and every time I read it, I would have things to add and remove. I wanted to sound really strong. I wanted the reader to want to do something about it. I want them to feel like the way I do, I want them to put themselves in my position.

One of the pieces that wasn't so effective was my vignette. I think people didn't really get the message I was trying to say. I was trying to say that racism is not a good thing and no matter what, don't say anything racist, because if you don't want people to be racist to you then don't do it to anyone else!!!

While I was writing "Come Home Now!" I got to really know about curfews. Teens all over the world have different curfew. Some have to go home right after school. And some can go home whenever they want. I discovered that some people have more freedom than others. And those who have freedom abuse it. In my article I would say that the "What Can We Do?" section was the best. My most lively sentence was "Take a stand. Don't let the government take away your rights."

In my notebook I recorded an interview that I used for my article. I interviewed my sister. She had lots to say about curfews, since she has none. I used information I think was important. In my writer's notebook, I have many pages about journalism. Throughout the month I have been taking notes. On February 14, 2006, I wrote about curfews. I asked questions I really needed to ask. And I planned to use my resources.

I made my sentences shorter but powerful. Instead of writing in the first person, I spoke in the third person. Instead of saying "I," "me," "my," or "you," I substituted those for "they," etc. Making my article more powerful.

If I had to do this assignment again, I would do a topic I actually enjoyed doing. I would try to work very hard doing it. Many students wrote about what they think was important. In our school we are getting a lot of sex education. So many teens in the world don't get the sex education they did. Therefore, they are most likely not to know about safe sex and that increases their chance to get a STD/STI or HIV/AIDS.

I didn't make any spelling errors, but I did make some sentences that didn't really make sense. I noticed myself writing unnecessary words and sentences. My sentences needed to be reworded. I had pretty good punctuation. Many of the mistakes were grammar mistakes.

This year I was never absent. I attended class 100 % of the time. I was hardly ever late. My materials, notes, and work are neat and organized. I always do my homework. I don't usually ask questions but when needed then I ask. I don't go to after school because when I am home I work better and I can concentrate better. But when really needed, I'll stay.

Next year I want to do better. Head for a 100, not only in humanities but also in my other subjects. I want to be able to concentrate on my work instead of getting distracted.

Sincerely,
Nazia Kamruzzaman

10th Grade June 7, 2007

Dear Reader,

"In the world of the near future, who will control women's bodies?" Women in this world are considered as people who are just useful for only reproduction. In *The Handmaid's Tale* by Margaret Atwood, she shows the way women could be treated in the future. It shows how women are tested for their strengths in daily life. While I read this book I was amazed to see what imagination can do and what a masterpiece it can create. I remembered thinking how outrageous everything sounded, but then as you start to think about it, everything starts to makes sense. You see that in reality everything is like what Margaret Atwood was writing and imagining, even though women aren't treated with equality and given the freedom to choose what they want. Reading this book made me deeply think of what this world is really like. Are they trying to take women's rights away? Or is this just a fear I have of losing the rights I have as an individual and not having the right to control what happens to my body? As a reader I love to read fiction, fiction that has to do with everyday life of a teen and what experiences they have to go through. I have read over 30 books. Reading keeps my mind at peace, when I am frustrated I can read a book and forget about all of my problems. This semester we read *Animal Farm* by George Orwell, we wrote anthologies (poems), we read and acted out scenes in Shakespeare's play, *Romeo and Juliet*, and many other things. I am writing this cover letter to let you know what kind of effort, and how much emotions and hard work I have put into our work this year, especially the second semester. I want you to think about how much English class means to us.

Throughout the whole year in English we had independent reading. Independent reading is a time in class where every student reads for thirty minutes or more. We are allowed to choose the book of our choice. It is important for the student to be able to read the book of their choice, because a reader should be able to get involved with their book. They should be able to be in the place of their character. If we don't like the book we are reading, we can always abandon it. Before we can go through this process, we really have to give this a second thought, is this the kind of book U want to read or am I just reading it because I have to? Reading matters to me because while reading a person does not have to worry about themselves, they can put themselves in the position of their character and feel their pain, joy, or sorrow instead of their own. Sometimes a reader can use some decisions the character made in their life and use it to apply it to your own life. This year I had a goal. Throughout the whole year I was reading average level books and I wanted to read a book that would challenge me. I finally was able to reach that goal. This year I have made progress as a reader. I know this because I pushed myself to read difficult, college level books, and I accomplished what I was set out to do, which was completing the book. I know last year I was not able to do it because I did not push myself hard enough as I have done this year, I read 31 books this year. I knew the minimum amount this year was to read 30 books, but I actually didn't know how many books to read until I counted them. I didn't let the numbers stop me from reading how many books I can read. I just read throughout the year on my own pace and I am proud to say I read

31 books. One reading strategy I used was how to pick a book and how many pages to read at a time. This strategy I had learned a long time ago, which I still use. As a reader I am very picky. When I choose a book to read, everything comes into play, such as the cover, title, the number of pages, the blurb, the themes, etc. Basically the book has to meet a certain criteria or else the book will not be on my list. This reading strategy comes into play any day of the year or whenever I have to choose a book. Every book that I select is really special to me and it always connects to my life one way or another. If they are not connected to my life, they are connected to my heart. As a tenth grader English student, my reading stamina and my ability to understand a vast amount of vocabulary has improved. I know this because if you compare the books I read last year to those that I read this year, there is a big difference in the books that I chose. Last year I read books that were at a higher level. I didn't use a dictionary to figure out the meaning of certain words, I used context clues. My reading stamina has somewhat improved. I am able to read more in a short amount of time. I would have been able to read more if I had more time and if I had my day's schedule planned out. With extra curricular activities and homework from both school and extra classes I took, it was hard to read an hour a day when I didn't even have ten minutes to relax. I hope next year I will be able to maintain my after school schedule and homework time. There is a book I read this year titled *The Handmaid's Tale* by Margaret Atwood. This book had such a great impact on me. Even though this book is science fiction, it just made so much sense. I think the main idea of this book was to show how society viewed women. My favorite character was the main character of the book, Offred. Offred is not her real name. We don't get to know her real name because her name has been changed by the officials. In this book the women are only used as people who produce babies. Their main objective in life would forever be to make babies. Offred tries once a month to get pregnant but she fails every month. Her commander (the person who tries to get her pregnant and the other women pregnant) meets with her two to three times a week. In this room they play games such as Scrabble. Here was a time where he took her out, which was forbidden for the women to do. Offred once has her own life. A mom, a husband, and a child, but gradually she lost everything. First her job, her house, her family, and then her dignity. She is my favorite character because in the book we get to know her inner thoughts. She was thinking about where her husband was and where her mom and daughter were; whether they were alive or . . . dead. She finds out her daughter is alive and is shown a picture of her daughter. Her daughter has the same fate as her. One challenge I have for myself next year and in the summer is to have a better and faster pace while reading.

Reading as a class is very important because then every student is participating and paying attention to many vocabulary words and if a student doesn't understand a section in the book, there is always our teacher or peers to explain it to us. During the days that we read *Romeo and Juliet* we did many activities. We read the prologue word to word, line to line, and then punctuation to punctuation. We went into groups. We also read it all together and walked while reading it. The activity that stood out to me was when we read line for line of the words that of what the characters were saying. It let us put some emotion into the play, which made it fun. I think when we were reading every word it made every word seem important. Each word had its own meaning, but when they were put together it has its other meaning. Also when we read the lines of the prologue, it seemed like everyone was getting a chance to participate. While preparing to perform Act III, scene IV, I had to figure out how Lady Capulet should act. I didn't have enough to say, but because of my body posture and where I sat in the scene, everyone got to know what character I would be playing, and I think everyone got to knew why Lady Capulet would be sitting instead of standing and why Lady Capulet wouldn't hold Capulet's arm to show her love for him or why Lady Capulet would only look the men in the eye while talking to them. When Capulet said, "Go you to Juliet ere you go to bed," that showed that he was ordering Lady Capulet to do what he said. He didn't ask her, but he told her. While reading *Romeo and Juliet*, I circled words that I didn't understand. That really helped me because there was Ed and Jen who were there to help me, but also it was me who figured out what they meant using context clues. With all the scenes we had to read, we had to reread them in order to understand them more. When reading it at first, we hardly understood it, but then we got used to how Shakespeare wrote by reading it. My favorite character in this play was Juliet because she was scared that her parent would not accept Romeo. She wanted to forget who she was for the person she loved. In Act IV, scene III, the problem here is that Juliet feared for her life. She feared that Romeo would not be next to her when she woke up. She was scared that the plan Friar made would really be the plan to kill her. Along with the reading *Romeo and Juliet*, we also read *Animal Farm* by George Orwell. That book had pigs and horses, etc. for characters, but the main idea of the book was to show how people in society were treated just because they were different. It showed us an important part of history and the deceitful things some can do to others because of greed. This year I learned so much. I learned about characters, setting, literary devices, and poetic devices, etc. While playing a character, you cannot be yourself. You have to be the character, act the way they would act. The setting is important, for example, Romeo and Juliet (the movie) was remade many times. One was in the old times and one was made in the modern times in which they didn't use swords but guns. While reading these texts (*Romeo and Juliet* and *Animal Farm*), I noticed that we had to read between the lines. Not everything was said or done in the book or movie, but we still understood what the main purpose of everything was.

As a writer I know that fluent writers write with their heart and they always edit and revise their work. They always remember this step because it is an important part of the writing cycle. Writing workshop is a time in class that the student would free write or write about something Jen told us to. It's a time when writers can express their feelings toward something. A writer's notebook is where we take notes and where we write all our free writes. The writing cycle consists of collecting drafting, revising, editing, and publishing. While writing our anthologies, we had to write many poems so we can get ready to collect them for the next step, which was to revise them. When I was revising my poems, I took one poem and made into two powerful poems. After I revised my poems, I designed it and then published it. One thing that helped me grow as a more sophisticated writer was the editing part of the cycle. I noticed how one poem was split apart, making the poems much stronger. While writing a literary essay, I learned that we can state our opinions in it. That's what I did in the *Animal Farm* literary essay. By using evidence from the book to my essay it made it much more convincing. By adding the evidence from the book, it supported my thesis because it showed real proof as to what the whole essay was going to be about. I have grown more as a writer. I know this because I used more writing strategies. Effective writing partnership looks like a team where the other writer would correct, help their peers, and comment on their work. For example, my former writing partner told me she liked my memoir. That meant a lot to me. Throughout the year we had publishing celebrations for each piece of work we completed and published. Publishing celebrations are times that our writing is presented to the whole class. They would read our writing and write thoughtful comments. When receiving feedback, it makes me grow as a writer because that gives me the support and appreciation a writer needs. When giving feedbacks, it also helps me grow as a writer because it shows me what mistakes and strong points I made and helps me use my own advice to help me on my own exhibition. My greatest accomplishment as a writer this year was when my 7–8 grade teacher Elisa told me my writing from the eighth grade to the tenth grade grew tremendously. To have her say that took a lot of work, but it gave me the strength to go on and write more powerful things that would allow people to understand me not only as a person but as a writer.

At the beginning of the poetry unit, I really liked writing poetry but as the unit was ending, I noticed that I was inspired by poetry and I also loved poetry. The strategies I used to me include poetic devices in revisions and final drafts were proofread and reread sentence and what I needed to add came automatically. Rereading really helps because it allows you to change and add things that were never there before. The significance of the BAM Poetry 2007 Performance was that many cultural were presenting their work and each had their own interpretation. We were able to see how each culture thought differently. Creating my anthology took a lot of patience, thought, and creativity. The length of the poem came into play, meaning if the poem was more than one page, it would have a different structure. My way of working includes lots of color, designs, different kinds of materials and mediums. The mood determined the way the poem would be presented. For example, if one of the poems were sad, the colors would be less bright. Basically the finished product was a process that was very well organized. I am proud of the fact that I never knew I could write such emotion-filled poems that reflect my life. When I reread them, I didn't recognize I was capable of this kind of work. This anthology showed that I was slowly becoming a poet, therefore I am proud of the entire anthology rather than just part of it. The poem that I read at the art gallery was chosen by my friends because I wanted their opinion on the one that stood out the most. By my friends choosing the poem, it made my decision much easier. The experience I had performing was interesting because while reading my poem, I was able to see the different expressions that people had. The strategies that I used to perform was putting emphasis on certain words that need it more than others, I learned that next time I should project my voice and speak at an understandable pace so the audience will catch on and be on the same page as me.

This event added to the many other wonderful experiences I had with East Side Community High School. This event was a way to help me present myself and share with the audience a bit about my work. This year I had a goal for myself. I wanted to learn to be strong throughout every obstacle in life. I mean in reality education as well. Life is too short to waste it on unimportant things, so I think we should live life to the fullest and make a mark in this world so that we will be remembered forever even though we won't live in this world forever.

Sincerely,
Nazia Kamruzzaman

11th Grade February 11, 2008

Dear Reader,

This past semester in English class was interesting and informative. We read novels that were interesting and could be connected to our lives. We read *Bodega Dreams* by Ernesto Quinonez, *Kindred* by Octavia Butler, *To Kill a Mocking Bird* by Harper Lee, and many other short stories. We wrote essays in class that compared many different ideas such as empowerment & exploitation, indoctrination & code switching, and apathy & inequality. By comparing two different texts we established a sense of understanding through analyzing. There were three major units this past semester: Community Leadership and Identity, Revolutionary Literature, and Searching for Justice in American Literature. We had exhibitions at the end of each unit to demonstrate that understanding. The Community Leadership and Identity unit mostly focused on *Bodega Dreams* and how it depicted issues of identity, leadership, exploitation, and empowerment in Spanish Harlem. The Revolutionary Literature unit focused on *Kindred* and how concepts of indoctrination and code switching were connected to revolutionary ideas that were exposed in *Kindred*. The Searching for Justice in American Literature unit focused on *To Kill a Mockingbird* and how individual rights of Americans were restricted or granted and what the relationship between apathy and inequality was, as expressed in several literatures. I am satisfied and proud of the work I completed the first semester. Each piece of work I completed followed the writing cycle. I brainstormed ideas, drafted, edited, revised, and published my work. We presented our work with our fellow peers and were critiqued on it. I am also proud of my work habit in this class. I was able to complete my homework every day with understanding and a lot of analyzing. I tried very hard to compose each piece of work. I worked diligently to exceed the level of expectations each work required.

The first unit focused on Community Leadership and Identity. We connected the topic to *Bodega Dreams* by Ernesto Quinonez. *Bodega Dreams* depicted issues of identity, leadership, and dreams in East Harlem. It showed how leadership came along with the exploitation of the people in East Harlem. Bodega showed that he could only empower his community by exploiting them. It showed how dreams for a neighborhood came with a price and that loyalty wasn't something everyone lived up to. Bodega was known as someone you can depend on for support. The fine line between empowerment and exploitation was expressed in relation to leadership in literature. With the reading in class, I was able to understand that there were positive ways and negative ways to express leadership. For example, in *Bodega Dreams*, Bodega was a leader but he was leading and empowering people by exploiting the communities. Also in "The Lesson" (one of the readings), Miss Moore had been the leader of her "kids." She set a good example to them by showing them what the worth of a dollar was for "minorities" and the hard work it took to earn it. While creating my own story about a community leader, I followed a specific process and short-story structure. I brainstormed ideas on how I wanted my character to act upon difficult situations. While completing my story structure, I started off with the exposition, then rising action before filling in the initial conflict, then moving onto the climax, which led to the falling action, eventually leading to the conclusion. My story showed how my character empowered his players with harsh rules that would be helpful to them throughout life. The unit was filled with many different situations, but they were all connected to one theme, the theme of either exploiting or empowering. The unit taught us a valuable lesson of what society and the community brings.

The second unit focused on Revolutionary Literature. We connected the topic to *Kindred* by Octavia Butler and other different genres of literature. In "Dear Mr. President," Pink uses a song to convey revolutionary messages. Langston Hughes uses various poems to convey his revolutionary messages; "The Boondocks" depicted a revolutionary message in a funny way. The students in our class wrote various things like poems, comic strips, etc. to show their revolutionary message. Indoctrination and code switching are connected to the revolutionary ideas as expressed in *Kindred*. *Kindred* showed how Dana has changed her habits and manners in order to live in the 1800s. She had to change the way she talked, dressed, and she had to learn to work and how to serve. She was to call all white people either master or ma'am. She had to wear dresses to "fit-in." She had to serve Rufus and her master, as well as the others because she was black. The major exhibition for this topic was to create a revolutionary message. We could express it through artwork, poems, letters, etc. I picked a revolutionary topic that was close to my heart, I chose to do a poem because my poems are expressive. I also created a little piece of artwork that showed the audience actual pictures of my topic, which where child soldiers.

The third unit focused on the Search of Justice in American Literature. We connected the topic to *To Kill a Mockingbird* by Harper Lee. Literature can show the different ways people struggle for justice. It shows the different ways people are wrong in societies and the great lengths they go to get justice. In *To Kill a Mockingbird*, individual's rights of Americans were restricted. Tom Robinson's rights were taken away when he was convicted guilty for raping Mayella Ewell. Tom Robinson did not rape her and it wasn't possible. Although evidence was given to the court proving Tom Robinson's innocence, he was still considered guilty because he was black and was convicted to a life sentence in prison. The texts that were shown to us revealed a relationship between apathy and inequality. The relationship between apathy and inequity are people who are apathetic do not care about things, and inequity is when things are unequal because of gender, race, or money. *To Kill a Mockingbird* showed both inequity and apathy because Tom Robinson was sent to jail because of inequity, and when Mr. Ewell falsely accused Tom that he raped his daughter, it was an example of apathetic situations.

Essay writing seems like a very hard thing to do, but all it takes are the right steps. Essays have a format and as long as you flow with that format, you are on the right track to an informative and thoughtful essay. When I first started to write essays, I started out on a three level (out of six). As I practiced more and more, my essay grade started to increase. I finally understood that essays are all about analyzing and showing understanding with evidence. I started to analyze more and find appropriate quotes for each essay. I followed the format and finally received a six. I did it. I was able to write an essay that included everything a level six essay should include.

This semester I was really interested as a reader because there were so many varieties of books that were available. I went to the National Teachers Convention and talked about bringing a reader and how East Side is a school where every student is required to read. After the presentation, we went to a book fair. I was able to get an advanced copy of many books. I even got autographs from some authors. The books I received were really inspiring books. They were all different genres, but they seemed to catch my attention. Unlike last year, I am able to read books that are very different genres. As I've mentioned earlier, we read many books as a class such as *Bodega Dreams*, *Kindred*, and *To Kill a Mockingbird*. My favorite book was *Bodega Dreams* because the character of Chino was an individual that I felt was a person that a lot of people could relate to. He reminds me of people I know, I like how Ernesto Quinonez depicts Chino as a person we all have inside of us. I feel as if Chino was our conscience.

I had a very good experience this semester. Kim presented different texts and materials. We started off the school year with "A Day without a Mexican" and continued to view other materials like the "Boondocks," and clips from the movie, "To Kill a Mockingbird." It was a different way of teaching and gave us a different kind of way of understanding and analyzing things. I enjoyed clips from the movie "To Kill a Mockingbird" because to tell you the truth, Scout was a really cute and innocent girl. I thought she really looked adorable in her ham costume. I would like to view more clips or movies and other materials that are work-related. It's good to have materials that make the class fun and interesting.

Sincerely,
Nazia Kamruzzaman

12th Grade January, 2009

Dear Reader,

There are very few classes and teachers that stand out throughout a student's life. AP English has taught me so many new things. Though the work we have done has been intense and has pushed us to our limit, it has taught us many things. Learning new terms, having vocabulary quizzes (very often, I must say), timed essays, essays, and tests, etc. You name it, we've done it already. I must confess, from the moment I was accepted into AP English, I started to worry. I did not know what to expect. So many questions started to fill my mind. How am I going to be able to manage my time? How am I getting to be able to pass this class? What if I don't pass? Will I be able to go to college? Oh my god, what is happening to me? Soon after, I started to feel sick to my stomach. Even before school officially *ended*, I had loads of homework. At first, I felt overwhelmed; I started to strongly dislike (hate!!!) the books Kim assigned us. She gave us *The Laramie Project* by Moises Kaufman and *Things Fall Apart* by Chinua Achebe. I remember sitting in the plane two days after school officially ended (I was on my way to Bangladesh) reading the first page of *Things Fall Apart* and I remember myself saying, "This is the worst book Kim has ever given us." Then I started to read *The Laramie Project*. I also really didn't like it. Honestly, I did not start *Things Fall Apart* till the middle of my vacation. But I had a really good excuse for that; I was sick for about two weeks. But I guess after my recovery, I should've started my assignment, but I didn't. After forcing myself to read, I actually started to like *Things Fall Apart*. I was blown away with the message the book had and the way the author conveyed it. I came back to America on August 13. I finished reading *The Laramie Project*, studying the 40+ vocabulary she gave us and writing a comparative essay. I did all of that within three weeks. I was officially ready for AP English.

I love AP English. The units we studied were something we could all relate to: tragedy, spoken word (poetry), and gender roles. Throughout this semester I encountered various genres in texts. By engaging myself in these texts, I was able to gain a different outlook that impacted my thinking process; it empowered me to question things in order to get a possible answer. I never knew I had the capacity to take on such rigorous readings. Every day, I challenged myself and pushed myself to digest as much as I could from the readings that were assigned. During the time so far in this class, I reached a level that I never thought I could surpass; I was able to be consistent in all my classes and homework assignments. Being consistent gave me a kind of pleasure in the sense that I knew I was able to produce great work at reasonable speed and time. I was appreciative of the types of strategies and explanations the teacher gave the class in order to have a better understanding of the subject. She made the class interesting to the point where I forgot this class was supposed to be difficult. We read *Antigone* by Sophocles for the tragedy unit. *Antigone* was a short story that showed how men portrayed women and what stereotypes are put upon them. *Antigone* was a story that showed the truth about society and its harsh gender rules that are made for women. *Antigone* revealed that when women surpass stereotypes, they are often dishonored and disrespected. They are labeled as "disrespectful" only because they have dared to step up. We learned some new terms for the unit, too. We leaned the word epiphany. I feel that this word has so much meaning and significance to it. I have not only used it in class, but also used it for my college essay. This word has given me more in-depth understanding of people, their actions, and why it is important to have an epiphany. It is important because it is then that people realize things and what was once unknown to them. I myself have experienced epiphanies, and I must say that they have shaped my life so much and have impacted it in great ways.

Another unit that I really liked and felt like I had a better understanding of was the unit we just finished. We were learning about gender roles. We watched the movie *Real Women Have Curves* and read the book *Their Eyes Were Watching God* by Zora Neale Hurston and *A Thousand Splendid Suns* because I felt I could connect to it. The book took place in Afghanistan, a predominantly Muslim country. I am also Muslim and from a predominantly Muslim country. I know what it feels like to be pressured into marriage and having to deal with things women cannot do because of their culture or religion. I feel that Khaled Hosseini portrayed those limitations very well by using actual events that happened in Afghanistan and how that affected the women. The connections and feelings I have toward books like *A Thousand Splendid Suns* help me learn and help me understand concepts such as why sexism exists and why women are constantly put down and omitted from doing things. Men are given the freedom to do whatever they want and this is somehow justifiable, but when women do it, it's considered a sin. I ask why. Why does this happen? This happens because of society and the unfair rules that are made to make men seem like the more superior gender. The belief that men are the superior gender degrades women and makes them feel like they are nothing; that they are just a piece of rag. This message was beautifully portrayed by Khaled Hosseini, and I have leaned so much from this one book. I have always loved the books Kim has assigned us, and I know that the books we will read in the future will be as magnificent and thoughtful as the books I have read before in Kim's class. Kim is my favorite teacher and I love her so much. I have learned so much from her class, and she has a very good sense of humor. Yes, her jokes are corny and lame sometimes (just kidding!!!), but I have grown to accept her jokes and her style of teaching and connecting with her students. Having Kim as a teacher for two years has been such an honor, and I hope that in college I will have professors that are just like Kim: thoughtful and dedicated. (P.S.–She writes a heck of a college recommendation.)

Sincerely,
Nazia Kamruzzaman

Handout 5.1

Eleventh-Grade English
End-of-Year Panel Presentation

CALL FOR PROPOSALS

The Power to the People Film Company is looking for the following screenplay proposals:

1. Stories with a science fiction angle that expose the realities of indoctrination in regards to race through the history of the United States. (*Kindred*)

2. Complex stories in which disillusioned characters struggle with individual versus collective power and hate. (*The Laramie Project*)

3. True life stories that depict how the failure of government services led to the disenfranchisement of certain people or a community. (*All Souls*)

4. An urban street story that examines the fine line between empowerment and exploitation. (*Bodega Dreams*)

This final panel presentation will be a group-produced screenplay proposal and will count as your roundtable for eleventh-grade English. Though your presentation will consist of group work, you will each have individual responsibilities.

- Typed description of the movie plot organized into three paragraphs as follows: Paragraph 1: The setup—where they are, the major characters, and the major conflicts; Paragraph 2: The action—major events that happen; Paragraph 3: The resolution—how it all comes to an end.
- Typed letter with three paragraphs: Paragraph 1: why this movie should be made and why people will go see it; Paragraph 2: how does this movie fulfill one of the stories the company is looking for (from list above); Paragraph 3: bankable elements—what stars you have lined up to be in the movie and why they will be good.
- Three-page typed scene (using screenplay format): Use one powerful event from the book and make it into a movie scene—it should show what is being asked for in the call for proposals.
- Video recording of the scene

Day of Presentation

➢ The letter will be read aloud.

➢ The scene will be introduced in context.

➢ Video recording will be shown.

➢ Question-and-answer session will be held.

Example 5.1

Written by Jonathan Back

ACT ONE:

Bodega Dreams takes place in Spanish Harlem. The main characters are Bodega, Chino, Sapo, Nazario, Vera, and Blanca. Bodega is a drug lord whose purpose in life is to empower and improve the Latino community. The movie follows the life of Chino as he gets involved in the drug business with Bodega. Sapo is Chino's childhood best friend and is the person who introduces Chino to Bodega. Nazario is Bodega's right-hand man. Vera is a past lover of Bodega but left him because he was an unsuccessful man. Bodega was also a Young Lord in his early days and was not a success in the group. Most of the conflict revolves around Bodega. Bodega creates issues between Chino and his wife Blanca. In the end there is a conflict between Nazario and Bodega.

ACT TWO:

There are a lot of major events that take place in this book. It all starts when Sapo first introduces Chino to Bodega after Chino was asked to hold some drugs for Sapo until he returned to get them later. Another major event is when Bodega reveals his plan to use Chino by getting Blanca to tell Chino information about the whereabouts of Vera and how he could get in contact with her. Vera is then contacted and asked to attend a school presentation. There she is met by Bodega and he tries to relight the passion that they had once had. Bodega is given the chance to show her how much of a success he has become, and they get back together to explore the wonders of the city together. Meanwhile, tensions fly between Chino and Blanca when Blanca continues to question Chino on his whereabouts every night and why he is beginning to change. She gets fed up with asking and asking and decides it's best for her to go live with her mother for a while in order to give him a message and allow him to get his life back in order. Sapo gets himself into deep trouble and goes on the down low when he kills a man named Alberto Salazar who made a deal with a rival of Bodega named Fischman.

ACT THREE:

The problems all end with the sudden death of Bodega. The plan is revealed at the end when it becomes clear that Nazario murdered Bodega and was with Vera the whole time. After the death of Bodega, things seem to go back to the way they were before Bodega started improving the community. All the people that Bodega helped are devastated but look ahead to a new beginning with their new leader Nazario. Bodega's dream was to have peace and to influence the Spanish community that they can become whatever they want. Nazario wanted the power to control this and have the same amount of respect that Bodega had in the community. Things begin to cool down with some of the lesser characters. Chino and Blanca seem to be patching things up as they begin to talk again after a long period of silence between the two. The community goes back to the way it was and do not expect the same treatment that Bodega gave with Nazario. After the death of Bodega, things change dramatically because Bodega is no longer around to control the power of the drug business and not letting it overtake the community. Bodega's dream was lived until his death.

Example 5.2

Written by Phillip Rodriguez

To the Power to the People Film Company:

Throughout the years, drugs, violence, and criminal activities have been glorified. Classics like "Scarface," The "Godfather" trilogy, and "Goodfellas" never really showed the other side of the lifestyle. They put spotlights on the very few that make it on top in the criminal world—showing them with new cars, beautiful women, and tigers in their backyard. This indoctrinates the viewers into believing this is the outcome from being a dealer, gangster, or a "menace to society." *All Souls*, on the other hand, if put on the screens, will portray the horror, showing people the truth about the outcomes of drugs in a community for the majority of the people. This can be a movie that can open eyes, helping people face or discover the truth. Furthermore it's based on a true story so it will be a touching movie that many can relate to. This movie will be guaranteed an Oscar if made. For the elders, it can be reflective experience, and for the younger ones, they can learn the ills of the past. The reality is the majority of people will find a way to connect to the MacDonald family.

Not only would this be a great movie to watch, but it will expose viewers to the truth. It will show how bad choices made by some family members in conjunction with some social service systems failing the family and the community led to many devastating results. It will make people think about the decisions they make and be aware of and look out for their local, state, or federal corruption. People will begin to understand that the government plays a part and role in why a certain type of people is poor. You can't ask for nothing better than a revolutionary and great movie. The movie will inspire people to want better for themselves, for their family, and for their community.

Actors have been calling me constantly begging us for roles. The one big name attached to the movie will be Robert DeNiro playing the role of the infamous Whitey Bulger. However, to be honest, this is the type of movie that doesn't even need to have famous actors in order for it to be good, and we will use many unknown and talented actors from the community in which it is set. This is just another way to empower a community that has been disenfranchised in the past.

Example 5.3

Written by Dolores Acosta

Fade In:

Ext. Hospital Room Day

(Kathy lying in hospital bed, Timmy and Julie enter the room and sit by her side.)

Michael
(V.O.)
Timmy always came to see Kathy, he wanted to be alone with her, always brought her flowers. He was known as the tough kid in Southie. In three years he will be found with two shots to the head in a car in front of the Quiet Man. Julie always came in high as kite, she was always crying, I couldn't tell if she was crying for Kathy or for herself. In a few years she will walk in the beach and would never come out.

(Frankie enters the room and sits by Kathy's bedside)

Michael
(V.O.)
I always felt weird when I was around Frankie. He gave me bad vibe. He was the one that got Kathy to use Angel Dust. Not long after this visit he will be found stabbed to death over a drug debt on Patterson Way.

(Tommy enters the room and sits next to Kathy.)

Michael
(V.O.)
Tommy always came to see Kathy, and when he did he would be dressing good for her. He would always crack jokes and laugh at his own joke. While Kathy would just be there lying and trying to survive. He would notice that cracking jokes wouldn't bring her back to life, so he would just quit joking and pray for her. In about two years he will be beaten to death by his girlfriend's family with a pipe.

(Okie comes in the room with Kevin; they both sit.)

Michael
(V.O)
Okie is a comedian says Frankie and Kevin, they always laugh when Okie says a joke or something. He's a coke addict, and Frankie is very worried about his coke use. Two years after this visit he will be found hanging from a rope in his parents' basement. He will only be 19 years old.

(Brian comes into the room and sits by Kathy's side.)

Michael
(V.O)
Ma met Brian when she started her internship at Suffolk University. He always liked her and enjoyed being around her so he started getting close to her. Not long after Ma starts her internship, Brian will get shot in the spine for breaking into a neighbor's house for drug money. He will be paralyzed

(Grandpa comes into the room and stands by Kathy's side.)

Michael
(V.O)
Grandpa came to Kathy that one day with Holy Water in one hand and a cross on the other. It was like magic. Once he threw Holy water at her, her hand moved. It was miracle. Kathy recovered slowly, and I realized that drugs weren't the way. I wanted to break the silence and denial in Southie. But that would take some time.

FADE OUT

Handout 5.2

QUESTIONS FROM THE PANEL:

Panelists can ask questions from this list or may ask questions that arise during "the pitch."

General Questions

- What is the message of this book—or what would be the message of this book as a movie? What did you take away from it as a reader, and what would viewers take away from it?
- You were able to choose from a variety of books and topics—why did you choose this one?
- How does the scene you chose depict the topic called for in the proposal?

Questions specific to novels:

- (*All Souls*) In regard to what the MacDonald family went through, were your assumptions challenged in any way because they are a white family, and do you think a movie audience would be challenged by this?
- (*Kindred*) Why do you think the author chose to move Dana from the 1970s, married to a white man, to the antebellum South? What is shown about the cycles of indoctrination / racism, and do these cycles still exist today?
- (*The Laramie Project*) What is the difference between collective and individual power, and how were the two negotiated in this text in relation to hate?
- (*Bodega Dreams*) Is Bodega a hero or a criminal—what should audiences believe? What did you believe? Bottom line—did he exploit his people or empower them?

Handout 5.3

Panelist Name: ______________________________

Group Members: ____

Proposed Book for Screenplay:

Please check if they address the following in their presentation:

___ Reasons people would want to see this movie.

___ Connection between text and topic: *All Souls* and disenfranchisement, *Kindred* and indoctrination, *Bodega Dreams* and empowerment / exploitation, *The Laramie Project* and disillusionment / hate.

___ Main plot points in the story.

While the students present and answer questions, please take notes in the following areas:

Notes / comments about STRENGTHS of the proposal and presentation.

Notes / comments about WEAKNESSES / QUESTIONS about the proposal and presentation.

OVERALL EVALUATION:

EXCELLENT **GOOD** **SATISFACTORY** **NEEDS WORK**

Works Cited

Allington, Richard. *What Really Matters for Struggling Readers*. Boston: Allyn & Bacon, 2006. Print.

Beers, Kylene. *When Kids Can't Read: What Teachers Can Do.* Portsmouth: Heinemann, 2002. Print.

Brozo, William. *To Be a Boy to Be a Reader: Engaging Teen and Preteen Boys in Active Literacy.* Newark, Del.: International Reading Association, 2002. Print.

Conley, David. *College Knowledge: What It Really Takes for Students to Succeed and What We Can Do to Get Them Ready.* San Francisco: Jossey-Bass, 2005. Print.

Crocco, Margaret, and Arthur Costigan. "The Narrowing of Curriculum and Pedagogy in the Age of Accountability." *Urban Education* 42.6 (2007): 512–535. Print.

Darling-Hammond, Linda. "Standards and Assessments: Where We Are and What We Need." *www.tcrecord.org*. Web. 2003.

Federman, Mark. "Literacy in the Middle School." Eds. D. Booth and J. Rowsell. *The Literacy Principal.* Portland: Stenhouse, 2007. Print.

———. "Developing and Sustaining an Adolescent Literacy Program at an Urban Secondary School." Harvard Institute for School Leadership. 8 July 2008. Address.

———. "Family Literacy." 1 September 2008. Address.

Fine, Michelle. *Framing Dropouts: Notes on the Politics of an Urban Public High School.* Albany: SUNY Press, 1991. Print.

Fine, Michelle, Lois Weis, and Linda Powell. "Communities of Difference: A Critical Look at Desegregated Spaces Created for and by Youth." *Harvard Educational Review* 67.2 (1997): 247–276. Print.

Greene, Maxine. "Imagining Futures: The Public School and Possibility." *Journal of Curriculum Studies* 33.2 (2000): 267–280. Print.

Huot, Brian. *(Re)Articulating Writing Assessment for Teaching and Learning.* Logan: Utah State University Press, 2002. Print.

Hursh, David. "The Growth of High-Stakes Testing in the USA: Accountability, Markets, and the Decline in Educational Equality." *British Educational Research Journal* 31.5 (2005): 605–622. Print.

Klein, Stephen P., Laura S. Hamilton, Daniel F. McCaffrey, and Brian M. Stecher. *What Do Test Scores in Texas Tell Us?* Santa Monica: The RAND Corporation, 2000. Print.

Koretz, David, and Sheila Barron. *The Validity of Gains on the Kentucky Instructional Results Information System (KIRIS).* Santa Monica: The RAND Corporation, 1998. Print.

Linn, Robert L. "Assessments and Accountability." *Educational Researcher* 29.2 (2000): 4–16. Print.

Meier, Deborah. *The Power of Their Ideas: Lessons for America from a Small School in Harlem.* Boston: Beacon, 2002. Print.

Meisels, Samuel, Sally Atkins-Burnett, and Yange Xue. "Creating a System of Accountability: The Impact of Instructional Assessment on Elementary Children's Achievement Test Scores." *Educational Policy Analysis Archives* 11.9 (2003). Print.

New York Performance Standards Consortium. "Parent Survey Report." *www.performanceassessment.org/consequences/cparents.html*. 2007. Web. 15 June 2009.

Perreault, George. "The Classroom Impact of High-Stress Testing." *Education* 120.4 (2000): 705–710. Print.

Plaut, Suzanne. *The Right to Literacy in Secondary Schools*. New York: Teachers College Press, 2009. Print.

Schmoker, Mike. "Measuring What Matters." *Educational Leadership* 66.4 (2008): 70–74. Print.

Tatum, Alfred. *Teaching Reading to Black Adolescent Males: Closing the Achievement Gap.* Portland: Stenhouse, 2005. Print.

The Teachers College Readers and Writers Workshop. "About Us." *http://rwproject.tc.columbia.edu/default.aspx?pageid=1076.* 2009. Web. 15 June 2009.

Wiggins, Grant. *Educative Assessment: Designing Assessments to Inform and Improve Student Performance.* San Francisco: Jossey-Bass, 1998. Print.

Wiggins, Grant, and Jay McTighe. *Understanding by Design*. Alexandria, VA: Association for Supervision and Curriculum Development, 1998. Print.

Index

"Accountable Talk," xiii
Achievement gap, curricula and, ix
Administrators, pressures on, viii
Allington, R. L., xiii, 5
Alternative assessments, xiv
Authentic assessment. *See also* Standardized tests
  curriculum focused on, ix
  defined, viii
  through differentiated reading conferences, 13–15
  importance of, 78
  plan for, 6–9
  prioritizing students in, 7
  recommendations for, 79–80
  of roundtables, 35
  site-based, 80
  time line for, 6
  voice and, 65–68
Authentic learning, viii

Backward curriculum planning, xiii
Beers, K., 4, 5
Biden, J., 77
Brozo, W., 4
Bush, G. W., 77

Confidence, importance of, 60
Conley, D., 27
Costigan, A., 81
Cover letters, 40–41, 49–51, 98–103
  examples of, 100–103, 113–28
  in high school, 49–51
  in middle school, 40–41
Crocco, M., 81
Curriculum, 63–65
  backward planning of, xiii, 63–64
  balancing with high-stakes testing, 68–70
  examining world through, 62
  focus on authentic assessment of, ix, 62
  integrating traditional assessments into, 70

Darling-Hammond, L., x
Debates, 53–54
Developmental Reading Assessment, 5
Differentiated reading conferences, 13–15

East Side Community High School (Manhattan), viii
  curriculum at, 63–76
  demographics of, viii–ix
  eleventh grade, 64–65
  quality review of, ix
English language arts (ELA) tests, xi

Families, empowering with reading data, 18
  ways to help children, 85–86
Federman, M., 3, 18, 22
Final project in independent reading, 19, 20–28
  analytical discussion, 25–26
  handout for, 21
  homework assignments for, 24
  pitfalls of, 26

preparation for, 20–21
soliciting facilitators for, 90
rationale for, 26–28
rubric for, 22
teacher modeling in, 25
Fine, M., 63, 68

Greene, M., 60, 63
Gross, L., 13

Habits, of successful independent readers, 6–7
Hamilton, L. S., xi
High-stakes tests
balancing assessments with, 68–70
pressures associated with, vii–viii
standards and, 77–78
Huot, B., 59, 80
Hursch, D., 77

Independent reading, xiii–xiv

as alternative to street life, 4
analytical discussion of, 25–26
authentic assessment of, 1–2, 19–28
benefits of, 1, 4
final project in, 19, 21–28
as graduation requirement, 19–28
in middle school classroom, 3–18
modeling of, 25
reading crisis and, 3–4
rubric for, 22
scaffolding of, 20–24

Keens, E., 5
Klein, S. P., xi
Kohn, A., viii, xii
Koretz, D., xi

Learning, viii
Libraries, classroom, 9–13
book bin labels for, 10–11
funding for, 12
Linn, R. L., xi

McCaffery, D. F., xi
McTighe, J., xiii, xiv, 64
Meier, D., 62
Meisels, S., 78
Michaels, S., xiii
Modeling, 25
Model passage, 87

New York City Department of Education, ix
New York Performance Standards Consortium (NYPSC), x, 35
No Child Left Behind
emphasis on standards of, 77
false assumptions of, xii

Obama, B., 30
O'Connor, C., xiii

Parents
empowering with reading data, 18
ways to help children, 85–86
Perreault, G., 81
Plaut, S., 62
Portfolios, xiv, 38–40
contents of, 38–40
high school, 51–52
middle school, 38–40
Presentation of skills, 52–54
Public speaking skills, 71

Reading. *See also* Independent reading
crisis in, 3–4
students' view of, 3
Reading circles, teacher, 5
Reading conferences, individualized, 13–15
prep sheet for, 84
Reading level
assessment of, 7–8
matching reading material with, 8, 11
Reading plans, 15–17
example of, 16–17
Reflective learners, nurturing, 59–61
Roundtables, xiv, 29
agenda for, 37, 94
cover letters for, 40–41, 49–51, 98–103, 106, 113–28

debate in, 53–54, 108
directions for students and visitors, 110
evaluation form for, 111
goals of, 35, 48–49
guest questions for, 38, 96, 112
guests for, 44–45, 105
in high school, 48–61
life lessons from 42–43
in middle school, 33–47
overview of, 37–38
personal reflection on, 30–31
portfolios, 38–40, 51–52
poster presentations, 41–42
preparing students for, 33–34, 49–54
presentation of skills, in, 52–54, 104
questions for discussion, 56–57
rubric for, 37, 56, 95–96
procedure for, 54–59
support for, 45–47
value of, 35–37

Scaffolding, providing structure for, 20–24
Schmoker, M., x
Screenplay panel presentation, 71–76
adapting to curriculum, 75–76
call for proposals, 128–32
choosing responsibilities in, 72
drafting and editing, 72–73
evaluation form for, 134
explaining project to students, 71–72
panelists for, 74–75
practice for, 73–74
questions from panel, 133
setup for, 74
Standardized testing
arguments for, xii
goals of, x
lower standards and, 77–78
parents' opinions on, xi–xii
pressures of, viii
validity of, x–xi
Stecher, B. M., xi
Students
pressures on, viii, 62
voice of, 65–68

Tatum, A., ix, xiii, 4, 15, 28, 30, 36
Teacher reading circles, 5
Teachers
assessment of, xi–xii
pressures on, viii
resources for, 5–6
Teachers College Fiction Reading Level Assessment, 8
Teachers College Reading and Writing Project, 5
Time constraints, 80–81

Voice, authentic assessment and, 65–68

Wiggins, G., viii, xiii, xiv, 52, 64, 78, 80
Word examiner lists, 7

Zelkha, S., 30
Zonana, E., 16

Authors

Joanna Dolgin teaches twelfth-grade English and journalism at East Side Community High School. She has developed a twelfth-grade curriculum for a differentiated classroom that emphasizes critical thinking and analytical writing for college readiness. She trained in inquiry education and alternative assessment at The Urban Academy Laboratory High School as a STEP/PONSI fellow. She received a master's degree in liberal studies from the Graduate Center of the City University of New York and her undergraduate degree from Yale University.

Kim Kelly is a New York City public school teacher of eleventh- and twelfth-grade English students and the high school department leader at East Side Community High School. She has been teaching in this system since 1996 and is dedicated to developing a curriculum around social, political, and emotional issues relevant to her students' lives. In addition to teaching, she has published a young adult novel, *L.E.S.: Love, Eloquence, and Stars*.

Sarvenaz Zelkha is a New York City public school teacher at East Side Community High School and has been teaching for eight years. She is an adjunct teacher for New York University and has presented for the National Council of Teachers of English and the Harvard Institute for School Leadership. She also runs workshops for NYC public school teachers in the Empowerment Network to help improve their independent reading curriculum.

This book was typeset in TheMix and Palatino by Barbara Frazier.

Typefaces used on the cover include Impact Regular, Frutiger Bold, Frutiger Light, and Helvetica Neue Standard.

The book was printed on 50-lb. Opaque Offset paper by Versa Press, Inc.